Bobby Iconic Recipes and Methods from a Modern Chef's Table Inspired by Flay Chapter 1 Cookbook

Culinary Inspirations behind the Flavors

"Bobby Iconic Recipes and Methods from a Modern Chef's Table Inspired by Flay Chapter 1 Cookbook"

Library of Congress Cataloging-in-Publication Data

Available upon request.

Contact Email: *mspublishing2003@gmail.com*

Cover Design by HS Publishers

Printed in USA

Table of Contents

Introduction: A Culinary Journey – The Making of Bobby Flay

Bobby Flay, a name that resonates deeply within the world of food, is more than just a celebrity chef. He represents a unique combination of raw passion, hard work, and an unrelenting drive to explore and push the boundaries of American cuisine. To understand Bobby Flay's culinary journey, we need to start with the basics of his upbringing, his influences, and his evolution into one of the most respected chefs in the world.

His story is one of inspiration, trial and error, and a never-ending pursuit of culinary excellence. Growing up in New York City, Bobby was always surrounded by food, but it wasn't until he began working in a local pizza parlor that he felt the spark of what would become his life's work. The restaurant world, with its challenges and rewards, became a space for him to hone his skills and forge his path.

The Creative Process Behind Each Dish

As you delve into the dishes Bobby Flay creates, it's clear that there is more to them than just ingredients. His creative process is deeply intertvinegard with his philosophy on food: simple, bold, and flavorful. Yet, there is also an underlying complexity in the way he combines these elements to create innovative and inspiring dishes.

Flay's ability to work with fire, his obsession with Southwestern flavors, and his respect for quality ingredients make his approach to cooking uniquely his own. His dishes, from the famous "Spice-Rubbed Beef Tenderloin" to the "Shrimp and Grits" he prepares on "Throwdown with Bobby Flay," are examples of how the creative mind works through trial, error, and reflection.

What makes Bobby Flay's process especially unique is his reliance on the rhythm of cooking. A dish is not just about the ingredients; it's about the feeling each dish evokes in the eater. Whether he's cooking on the grill, preparing a sauce, or picking out spices, Bobby Flay is always thinking about how the dish will come together in harmony to create an experience.

For Flay, the kitchen is a canvas, and the ingredients are the tools that bring the art to life. This philosophy drives his attention to detail and his constant search for new techniques, combinations, and inspirations. His love for bold flavors, especially his signature southwestern and Mediterranean influences, can be found in almost every dish he creates. His approach is the antithesis of formulaic; he embraces change, he evolves with the times, and he never lets himself get comfortable in his culinary mastery.

A Deep Dive Into Flay's Process

The creative process behind each dish begins well before Flay steps into the kitchen. Inspiration strikes from various sources—be it travels, cultural influences, or simply a flavor he's craving. He often reflects on ingredients he grew up with or experiences from his trips, often revisiting the foods of the American Southwest, where he found his signature style.

Flay's kitchen is a place where experimentation is not only allowed but encouraged. He's known for using heat in ways that can transform a dish. His love of grilling, whether it's steak, fish, or vegetables, comes from his desire to bring out the natural flavors of ingredients while adding layers of smoky complexity.

Take, for instance, his famous grilled lobster tail with ancho chile butter. It's a dish that exemplifies Flay's artistry: the sweetness of the lobster is perfectly balanced with the smoky heat of the ancho chile. This dish didn't come together in one sitting. It took trial and error, along with many nights of refining flavors, until Bobby was satisfied with the outcome.

Every dish Flay creates reflects his understanding of flavor layering, timing, and presentation. But it's also about his confidence in trusting his instincts and tasting along the way. For Bobby, cooking is not just following a recipe— it's an organic and adaptive process that comes alive with each step.

How to Use This Book: The Journey of Cooking Like Bobby Flay

This book is not just a collection of recipes or a tribute to Bobby Flay's remarkable career. It's a guide to understanding the philosophy and process that makes his cooking so special. It's a deep dive into his world, where you'll not only learn how to cook like Bobby Flay but also how to think about food with a similar sense of creativity and exploration.

Much like Bobby Flay approaches each dish with an open mind, this book invites you to do the same. It is about embracing cooking not as a rigid discipline but as an ongoing creative process. Whether you are new to the kitchen or an experienced home cook, Bobby Flay's methods will open new doors for you. You'll learn how to mix bold flavors, perfect your technique, and embrace the art of cooking.

A Personal Connection to the Kitchen

This book invites you to step into Bobby Flay's shoes—though without the years of culinary experience or the world-class kitchen. Think of it as a conversation with a chef who's been there, done that, and is now ready to share his knowledge, wisdom, and insights.

Bobby's culinary journey is more than just a professional one; it's personal. He's the kind of chef who truly invests in every dish he creates, considering not just the ingredients and techniques, but the emotional connection between food and the people who will enjoy it. Flay's personal stories—his rise to fame, his struggles in the kitchen, and the relationships he's formed with food over the years—are all woven into his cooking.

For example, Flay talks often about his love for Southwestern flavors, a passion that stems from his time in the Southwest, where he was inspired by the region's bold spices and techniques. His restaurant, Mesa Grill, has been a place of innovation, where dishes like his signature "Miso-glazed Salmon" are born from experimentation and his obsession with flavor combinations.

Flay has always believed that cooking is about forging personal connections with the ingredients you use and the people you cook for. It's a philosophy he shares throughout this book. As you begin your culinary journey, you'll see that cooking, for Bobby Flay, is not about simply following a recipe. It's about expressing your creativity, experimenting with flavors, and always trusting your instincts. You might not always get it right on the first try, but each attempt brings you one step closer to understanding the essence of what makes cooking an art form.

Breaking Down the Recipes

This book will feature recipes that range from Bobby's classic creations to new and inspired dishes that demonstrate his evolving approach to food. Each recipe comes with its own story, giving you a deeper understanding of why the dish exists and how it fits into Bobby's culinary philosophy. These are not just "step-by-step" recipes; they are blueprints for you to adapt, explore, and make your own.

Bobby's recipes are designed to be flexible, allowing for adjustments based on what you have in your kitchen or what ingredients you prefer. They encourage you to experiment with different flavors, substitutions, and techniques—just as Bobby himself does in his own kitchen. You might find that you prefer a different spice in a rub or swap out an ingredient for one that better suits your taste.

Cooking, according to Bobby Flay, is a personal journey, and this book aims to reflect that. Each dish tells a story. But your own story is just as important—what you bring to the table, how you experiment, and how you make each dish your own.

This introduction sets the tone for what could be an extensive exploration of Bobby Flay's culinary philosophy, his creative process, and the techniques that have made him a household name. It encourages readers to not just follow recipes but to embrace the art of cooking and the adventure that comes with it.

Chapter 1: Beginnings and Bold Flavors

Introduction: The Early Years of a Culinary Pioneer

Bobby Flay's culinary journey did not start in a state-of-the-art kitchen or in a prestigious restaurant. It began with humble beginnings in New York City, where he was exposed to food at a young age. His early passion for cooking was ignited while working at a pizza parlor, followed by stints at various restaurants in the city that helped shape his palate. Bobby's exposure to a wide range of flavors, from traditional American comfort foods to the bold spices of the Southwestern U.S., set the stage for his unique approach to cooking.

It was his exposure to the culinary diversity of the Southwest and his obsession with bold flavors that truly set him apart. From his early years working under other chefs to opening his own restaurants, Bobby learned the value of using fire and spice to create dishes that were as innovative as they were delicious.

King Crab Gumbo with Crab Rice and Crispy Okra

One of Bobby's standout dishes that has earned rave reviews from critics and fans alike is his *King Crab Gumbo with Crab Rice and Crispy Okra*. Inspired by his travels to the Gulf Coast, this dish reflects his love for seafood, bold spices, and his signature Southwestern flair.

Ingredients:

- **For the Gumbo:**
  - 2 tbsp olive oil
  - 1 large onion, chopped
  - 1 bell pepper, chopped
  - 2 celery stalks, chopped
  - 4 cloves garlic, minced

- o 1 1/2 tsp smoked paprika
- o 1 tsp dried thyme
- o 1/2 tsp cayenne pepper
- o 1/4 tsp ground black pepper
- o 1 bay leaf
- o 6 cups chicken stock
- o 1 1/2 lbs king crab meat (or a mix of crab if unavailable)
- o 1/4 cup Worcestershire sauce
- o 2 tbsp hot sauce (optional for extra kick)
- **For the Crab Rice:**
  - o 1 cup jasmine rice
  - o 2 cups crab stock (or seafood stock)
  - o 1/2 lb lump crab meat
  - o 1 tbsp butter
  - o Salt and pepper to taste
- **For the Crispy Okra:**
  - o 1 lb fresh okra, sliced into 1/2-inch rings
  - o 1 cup buttermilk
  - o 1 cup cornmeal
  - o Salt and pepper to taste
  - o Vegetable oil for frying

Preparation:

1. **The Gumbo:**
   - o Begin by heating the olive oil in a large Dutch oven over medium heat. Add the chopped onion, bell pepper, and celery, cooking for

6-8 minutes until softened. Stir in the garlic and cook for an additional 2 minutes.

o   Add the smoked paprika, thyme, cayenne pepper, black pepper, and bay leaf. Stir to combine and toast the spices for about 1 minute.

o   Slowly pour in the chicken stock, stirring to deglaze the pan. Bring the mixture to a simmer and let it cook for 25-30 minutes, allowing the flavors to develop.

o   Add the crab meat, Worcestershire sauce, and hot sauce. Simmer for an additional 5-10 minutes, just long enough to warm the crab through. Adjust the seasoning with salt and pepper to taste.

2. **The Crab Rice:**

o   In a saucepan, combine the rice and crab stock (or seafood stock). Bring to a boil, then reduce to a simmer and cover. Cook for about 15-18 minutes until the rice is tender and the liquid is absorbed.

o   Once cooked, fluff the rice with a fork and stir in the butter and lump crab meat. Season with salt and pepper.

3. **The Crispy Okra:**

o   Heat a large skillet with vegetable oil over medium-high heat. Place the sliced okra into a bowl of buttermilk, allowing it to soak for about 5 minutes. In another bowl, combine the cornmeal with salt and pepper.

o   Dredge the soaked okra in the cornmeal mixture and fry in batches until golden brown, about 3-4 minutes per batch. Drain on paper towels.

4. **Assembly:**

o   Serve the gumbo in large bowls, placing a scoop of crab rice in the center. Top with the crispy okra and garnish with freshly chopped parsley.

Tips & Tricks:

- **Balancing the Spices:** The balance between the smoky paprika, cayenne, and the sweetness of the crab is key. Taste as you go and adjust according to your preference.

- **Fresh vs. Frozen Crab:** Fresh crab meat is ideal for this dish, but if you're using frozen, make sure it's fully thawed and drained of excess liquid.

- **Crispy Okra:** Okra can sometimes become soggy if not fried properly. Make sure the oil is hot enough, and don't overcrowd the pan to ensure even frying.

Shrimp and Roasted Garlic Tamale

The *Shrimp and Roasted Garlic Tamale* is another one of Bobby's signature dishes, where he merges traditional Mexican flavors with an innovative twist. Tamales are a great vehicle for experimentation, and Bobby's version takes the traditional dish to new heights with the delicate sweetness of shrimp and the richness of roasted garlic.

Ingredients:

- **For the Tamale Dough:**
    - 2 cups masa harina
    - 1/2 cup vegetable oil
    - 1 tsp baking powder
    - 1 tsp salt
    - 1 1/2 cups chicken broth
    - 1/2 cup grated Parmesan cheese

- **For the Shrimp Filling:**
    - 1 lb shrimp, peeled and deveined
    - 6 cloves garlic, roasted and mashed

- o 1 tbsp olive oil
- o 1/2 tsp smoked paprika
- o 1/2 tsp cumin
- o Salt and pepper to taste
- o 1/4 cup chopped cilantro
- **For the Sauce:**
  - o 2 cups tomatillos, husked and roasted
  - o 1/2 cup green onions
  - o 1/4 cup fresh lime juice
  - o 1 tbsp honey

Preparation:

1. **Preparing the Tamale Dough:**
   - o In a large bowl, combine the masa harina, baking powder, salt, and Parmesan cheese. Gradually add the chicken broth and oil, mixing until a dough forms. The dough should be moist but not sticky.

2. **Preparing the Shrimp Filling:**
   - o Heat olive oil in a skillet over medium heat. Add the shrimp, roasted garlic, smoked paprika, cumin, and a pinch of salt and pepper. Cook until the shrimp turns pink and opaque, about 3-4 minutes. Remove from heat and set aside. Chop the shrimp into small pieces and stir in the chopped cilantro.

3. **Assembling the Tamales:**
   - o Take a small amount of masa dough and spread it onto a softened corn husk. Add a spoonful of the shrimp filling in the center, then fold the sides of the husk over to close the tamale. Repeat with the remaining husks and filling.

4. **Cooking the Tamales:**

- Place the tamales in a large steamer basket, standing them upright. Cover with additional corn husks and steam for 1 hour, or until the masa is fully cooked and has pulled away from the husk.

5. **Preparing the Sauce:**

   - Blend the roasted tomatillos, green onions, lime juice, and honey in a blender until smooth. Heat in a small saucepan before serving.

6. **Serving:**

   - Serve the tamales with the tomatillo sauce on top and a sprinkle of fresh cilantro.

Tips & Tricks:

- **Tamale Dough Consistency:** The masa dough should feel soft but firm enough to hold together. If it feels dry, add a little more chicken broth.

- **Roasting Garlic:** Roasting garlic enhances its natural sweetness. Wrap the garlic cloves in foil and roast them at 400°F for 20 minutes.

- **Filling Options:** You can substitute shrimp with chicken or vegetables for a different variation.

Mesa Grill's Spicy Grilled Chicken Nachos

One of Bobby's hallmark dishes, *Spicy Grilled Chicken Nachos*, is a fusion of bold Southwestern flavors and comfort food. The combination of spicy grilled chicken, melted cheese, and crunchy tortilla chips makes this dish irresistible.

Ingredients:

- **For the Grilled Chicken:**

  - 4 boneless, skinless chicken breasts
  - 2 tbsp olive oil
  - 1 tbsp chili powder
  - 1 tsp cumin

- o 1/2 tsp cayenne pepper
- o Salt and pepper to taste
- o 1 tbsp lime juice
- **For the Nachos:**
  - o 1 bag of tortilla chips
  - o 2 cups shredded cheddar cheese
  - o 1 cup shredded Monterey Jack cheese
  - o 1/2 cup sliced jalapeños
  - o 1/4 cup chopped red onion
  - o 1/4 cup fresh cilantro
- **For the Toppings:**
  - o 1 cup sour cream
  - o 1/4 cup hot sauce

Preparation:

1. **Grilling the Chicken:**
   - o Marinate the chicken breasts in olive oil, chili powder, cumin, cayenne pepper, lime juice, salt, and pepper for at least 30 minutes. Preheat a grill or grill pan over medium-high heat.
   - o Grill the chicken for 6-8 minutes per side until fully cooked. Slice the chicken thinly once cooked.

2. **Assembling the Nachos:**
   - o Preheat your oven to 375°F. On a large baking sheet, arrange the tortilla chips in a single layer. Layer with the grilled chicken, cheddar cheese, Monterey Jack cheese, jalapeños, and red onions.
   - o Bake for 10-12 minutes until the cheese is melted and bubbly.

3. **Topping the Nachos:**

- Remove from the oven and top with fresh cilantro, a dollop of sour cream, and a drizzle of hot sauce.

Tips & Tricks:

- **Grill Marks:** To get those beautiful grill marks on your chicken, make sure the grill is hot before placing the chicken on it.

- **Crunchy Nachos:** Bake the nachos on a sheet of parchment paper to keep the chips from becoming soggy.

- **Make it Spicy:** Add more jalapeños or a sprinkle of chili flakes for extra heat.

These recipes are just the beginning of a journey into Bobby Flay's kitchen and his approach to bringing bold flavors to life. Each dish combines layers of personal experience, passion for the craft, and a commitment to using the best ingredients to create something unforgettable. As you work through these recipes, keep in mind that Bobby's cooking philosophy isn't about following rules—it's about experimenting, tasting, and finding your own voice in the kitchen.

Chapter 2: The Art of Southwestern Cooking

Introduction: Finding Inspiration in the Southwest

The Southwest is a place where land, culture, and food intersect. From the rich, smoky chiles to the robust spices and fresh, local ingredients, the Southwest has long inspired chefs, including Bobby Flay, who was drawn to this region for its complex flavors and culinary history. What makes Southwestern cooking so compelling is the deep connection to the land and the people who have shaped the culinary traditions of this region. Flay, with his passionate approach to food, found himself at home in the Southwest, where he could draw from his experiences and develop dishes that balance heat, complexity, and unexpected flavor combinations.

Southwestern cuisine is all about boldness—bold flavors, bold ingredients, and bold techniques. The use of chile peppers, smoked spices, fresh herbs, and a strong reliance on grilling and slow cooking set the stage for an exciting journey through these recipes. In this chapter, we'll explore some of Bobby's signature Southwestern dishes that reflect both his personal evolution as a chef and his unwavering dedication to the flavor profiles of this region.

Southwestern Caesar Salad

A playful twist on the classic Caesar salad, the Southwestern Caesar is Bobby Flay's take on a dish that has been beloved for generations. By incorporating the bold and smoky flavors of the Southwest, this salad comes alive with rich, flavorful ingredients.

Ingredients:

- **For the Dressing:**
    - 1/2 cup mayonnaise
    - 2 tablespoons lime juice

- 2 teaspoons chipotle chile in adobo, minced
- 1 teaspoon Dijon mustard
- 1/2 cup grated Parmesan cheese
- 2 tablespoons olive oil
- Salt and pepper, to taste

- **For the Salad:**
  - 2 hearts of romaine lettuce, washed and chopped
  - 1/2 cup roasted corn kernels (fresh or frozen)
  - 1/2 cup tortilla strips, fried or store-bought
  - 1/4 cup crumbled queso fresco
  - 1 avocado, sliced
  - 1 tablespoon chopped cilantro (optional)

Preparation:

1. **Making the Dressing:**
   - In a bowl, whisk together the mayonnaise, lime juice, chipotle chile, Dijon mustard, Parmesan cheese, and olive oil. Season with salt and pepper to taste. Adjust the consistency by adding a little more lime juice or olive oil if needed.

2. **Assembling the Salad:**
   - Toss the romaine lettuce, roasted corn, tortilla strips, and avocado in a large bowl. Drizzle the dressing over the salad and toss to coat.
   - Garnish with crumbled queso fresco and chopped cilantro.

Tips & Tricks:

- **Adjusting Heat:** The chipotle in adobo can be adjusted based on your spice tolerance. Start with a little and add more if you want an extra kick.

- **Roasting Corn:** If you're using fresh corn, grill or roast it for added flavor. Frozen corn works well too, but roasting it on a hot pan can replicate the smoky taste.

Grilled Rib-Eye with Spicy Adobo Marinade

Rib-eye steaks are a fan favorite for their tenderness and rich flavor. Bobby Flay takes this classic steak dish to new heights by marinating the meat in a spicy adobo marinade that brings bold, smoky heat to every bite.

Ingredients:

- **For the Marinade:**
  - 3 tablespoons olive oil
  - 2 tablespoons red vinegar vinegar
  - 1 tablespoon chipotle in adobo sauce, minced
  - 1 tablespoon smoked paprika
  - 1 teaspoon ground cumin
  - 1 teaspoon dried oregano
  - 2 cloves garlic, minced
  - 1/4 cup fresh lime juice
  - Salt and freshly ground black pepper, to taste
- **For the Steak:**
  - 2 rib-eye steaks (about 1 1/2 inches thick)
  - Olive oil for grilling

Preparation:

1. **Making the Marinade:**

- In a bowl, whisk together the olive oil, red vinegar vinegar, chipotle in adobo, smoked paprika, cumin, oregano, garlic, and lime juice. Season with salt and pepper.

- Place the rib-eye steaks in a resealable plastic bag and pour the marinade over them. Seal the bag and refrigerate for at least 2 hours, preferably overnight.

2. **Grilling the Steak:**

- Preheat the grill to medium-high heat. Brush the steaks with olive oil to prevent sticking.

- Grill the steaks for 4-6 minutes per side for medium-rare, or longer depending on your preferred doneness.

- Let the steaks rest for 5 minutes before slicing.

Tips & Tricks:

- **Doneness Testing:** Use a meat thermometer to check for doneness— 130°F for medium-rare, 140°F for medium.

- **Enhance the Marinade:** If you like more depth in the marinade, add a tablespoon of honey or brown sugar to balance out the heat.

Red Chile and Blue Corn Enchiladas

These enchiladas showcase the distinct flavors of the Southwest, with the earthy blue corn tortillas and smoky red chile sauce creating a combination that's as bold as it is delicious.

Ingredients:

- **For the Red Chile Sauce:**

  - 6 dried ancho chiles, seeds and stems removed

  - 2 dried guajillo chiles, seeds and stems removed

  - 2 tomatoes, halved

- o 1/2 onion, quartered
- o 2 cloves garlic, unpeeled
- o 1 teaspoon ground cumin
- o Salt to taste
- o 4 cups chicken broth
- **For the Enchiladas:**
  - o 12 blue corn tortillas
  - o 2 cups cooked shredded chicken (or beef)
  - o 1 1/2 cups grated cheese (cheddar, Monterey Jack, or a mix)
  - o 1/2 cup chopped cilantro
  - o 1/4 cup sliced red onions
  - o Olive oil for frying

Preparation:

1. **Making the Red Chile Sauce:**
   - o Heat a dry skillet over medium heat. Toast the ancho and guajillo chiles until fragrant, about 2 minutes. Remove the chiles and set them aside to cool.
   - o In the same skillet, char the tomatoes, onion, and garlic until slightly blackened, about 5 minutes.
   - o In a blender, combine the toasted chiles, tomatoes, onion, garlic, cumin, salt, and chicken broth. Blend until smooth. Return to the skillet and simmer for 15 minutes until thickened.

2. **Assembling the Enchiladas:**
   - o Heat a small amount of olive oil in a skillet over medium heat. Lightly fry each tortilla for about 30 seconds per side to soften. Drain on paper towels.
   - o Preheat the oven to 375°F. Spread a thin layer of red chile sauce in the bottom of a baking dish.

- o Fill each tortilla with shredded chicken and cheese, roll them up, and place them seam-side down in the baking dish. Pour the remaining red chile sauce over the top and sprinkle with the remaining cheese.

3. **Baking:**

- o Bake for 20-25 minutes until the cheese is melted and bubbly.

Tips & Tricks:

- **Corn Tortillas:** Blue corn tortillas add a unique flavor, but if you can't find them, yellow corn tortillas work just as well.

- **Make it Vegan:** Substitute the chicken with black beans or roasted vegetables, and use dairy-free cheese for a plant-based version.

Roasted Corn and Poblano Queso Fundido

This dish is a cheesy, smoky delight, perfect for dipping tortilla chips or as a side to any Southwestern meal. Roasting the poblano peppers and corn brings out their natural sweetness, balancing the richness of the melted cheese.

Ingredients:

- 2 poblano peppers
- 1 cup roasted corn kernels
- 2 cups shredded Monterey Jack cheese
- 1 cup shredded cheddar cheese
- 1 tablespoon olive oil
- 1/4 cup chopped cilantro
- 1/4 teaspoon ground cumin
- 1/4 teaspoon smoked paprika
- Salt and pepper to taste

Preparation:

1. **Roasting the Peppers and Corn:**

   o Roast the poblano peppers over an open flame or under a broiler until charred. Place in a bowl and cover with a towel to steam. Peel off the skins, remove the seeds, and chop the peppers.

   o In a skillet, heat the olive oil and sauté the corn kernels until golden brown. Set aside.

2. **Assembling the Queso Fundido:**

   o Preheat your oven to 375°F. In an ovenproof dish, combine the roasted poblano peppers, sautéed corn, Monterey Jack cheese, cheddar cheese, cilantro, cumin, and smoked paprika. Season with salt and pepper.

3. **Baking:**

   o Bake for 15-20 minutes, or until the cheese is melted and bubbly. Serve hot with tortilla chips.

Tips & Tricks:

- **Smooth Cheese Melting:** Grate the cheese yourself rather than using pre-shredded cheese for the best melt.

- **Extra Heat:** Add some chopped jalapeños or a pinch of cayenne pepper for extra spice.

Charred Chile-Citrus Shrimp with Lime-Avocado Salsa

This dish is a perfect example of Bobby Flay's ability to balance heat and freshness. The charred shrimp are seasoned with a citrusy, smoky marinade, and the lime-avocado salsa adds a refreshing touch.

Ingredients:

- 1 lb large shrimp, peeled and deveined

- 2 tablespoons olive oil
- 2 tablespoons fresh lime juice
- 1 tablespoon orange juice
- 2 teaspoons smoked paprika
- 1 teaspoon ground cumin
- 1 teaspoon chili powder
- Salt and pepper to taste
- **For the Salsa:**
  - 1 avocado, diced
  - 1/2 cup diced tomatoes
  - 1/4 cup chopped red onion
  - 2 tablespoons chopped cilantro
  - 1 tablespoon lime juice
  - Salt to taste

Preparation:

1. **Marinating the Shrimp:**
   - In a bowl, combine olive oil, lime juice, orange juice, smoked paprika, cumin, chili powder, salt, and pepper. Add the shrimp and toss to coat. Let marinate for 15-20 minutes.

2. **Cooking the Shrimp:**
   - Preheat a grill or grill pan to medium-high heat. Grill the shrimp for 2-3 minutes per side, or until charred and cooked through.

3. **Making the Salsa:**
   - In a bowl, combine avocado, tomatoes, red onion, cilantro, and lime juice. Season with salt.

4. **Serving:**

o   Serve the charred shrimp with the lime-avocado salsa on top.

Tips & Tricks:

- **Perfect Grill Marks:** Make sure the grill is hot before adding the shrimp to get those beautiful char marks.

- **Avocado Substitute:** If you're not a fan of avocado, you can swap it out with diced mango or papaya for a sweeter contrast.

This chapter reflects the bold, dynamic flavors of Southwestern cuisine and Bobby Flay's personal culinary style. Each recipe offers a unique twist on classic dishes, blending heat, smoke, and fresh ingredients to create unforgettable meals. Whether you're grilling, roasting, or sautéing, these recipes allow you to explore the bold flavors of the Southwest from the comfort of your own kitchen.

Chapter 3: New American Classics

Introduction: Flay's Take on Modern American Cuisine

The evolution of modern American cuisine can be seen as a reflection of the country's diverse landscape and rich history. From regional specialties to fusion cuisines, American food has constantly been influenced by the many cultures that call this vast land home. In his approach to modern American cuisine, Bobby Flay redefines the idea of comfort food by blending bold flavors, creative techniques, and classic American ingredients with international influences. The result is a category of cooking that is uniquely American—innovative yet rooted in tradition.

Flay's "New American" philosophy is one of reinvention and excitement. As he draws from his love for bold Southwestern flavors, his extensive travels, and his deep respect for European techniques, he creates dishes that honor the past but embrace the future. He believes that food should not only be about nostalgia but also about pushing boundaries, challenging the palate, and creating memorable dining experiences.

This chapter celebrates Bobby Flay's take on New American classics. These are dishes that showcase the modern American chef's creativity, paying homage to traditional flavors and techniques while boldly reinterpreting them for today's contemporary tastes.

Black Rice Paella with Shellfish and Scallion Relish

Inspired by the traditional Spanish paella, Bobby Flay's version takes a unique turn with the use of black rice, often referred to as "forbidden rice." This dish is rich in color, flavor, and texture, featuring a combination of shellfish and a fresh, zesty scallion relish that adds a contemporary twist to this classic.

Ingredients:

- **For the Paella:**

- o 1 1/2 cups black rice (forbidden rice)
- o 4 tablespoons olive oil
- o 1 small onion, finely chopped
- o 4 cloves garlic, minced
- o 1 teaspoon smoked paprika
- o 1/2 teaspoon saffron threads
- o 2 cups chicken stock
- o 1 cup dry white vinegar
- o 1/2 pound shrimp, peeled and deveined
- o 1/2 pound mussels, scrubbed
- o 1/2 pound clams, scrubbed
- o 1/2 pound squid, cleaned and cut into rings
- o 1 tablespoon tomato paste
- o 1/2 teaspoon ground turmeric
- o Salt and freshly ground black pepper to taste
- o Lemon wedges, for serving
- **For the Scallion Relish:**
  - o 4 scallions, thinly sliced
  - o 1 small red chili, finely chopped (optional)
  - o 1 tablespoon lemon juice
  - o 1 tablespoon olive oil
  - o Salt and pepper to taste

Preparation:

1. **Cooking the Rice:**

- In a large paella pan or wide skillet, heat olive oil over medium-high heat. Add the chopped onion and garlic and cook until softened, about 3-4 minutes. Stir in the smoked paprika, saffron threads, and turmeric.

- Add the black rice and toast it lightly in the oil and spices for about 2 minutes. This step will enhance the flavor of the rice.

- Add the chicken stock and white vinegar, bring to a boil, then lower the heat to a simmer. Cover and cook for about 20 minutes, or until the rice is tender and has absorbed most of the liquid.

2. **Cooking the Shellfish:**

- While the rice is cooking, heat a separate skillet with olive oil over medium-high heat. Add the shrimp, mussels, clams, and squid to the pan, seasoning with salt and pepper. Sauté for 3-4 minutes, or until the shellfish is cooked through and the mussels and clams have opened up. Discard any unopened shellfish.

- Add the tomato paste to the shellfish and stir to combine, cooking for another minute. Remove from heat and set aside.

3. **Making the Scallion Relish:**

- In a small bowl, combine the sliced scallions, chopped chili (if using), lemon juice, and olive oil. Season with salt and pepper. Set aside to let the flavors meld.

4. **Assembling the Paella:**

- Once the rice is cooked, gently fold in the sautéed shellfish mixture. Stir carefully to combine, making sure not to break up the shellfish too much.

- Garnish the paella with the fresh scallion relish and serve with lemon wedges on the side.

Tips & Tricks:

- **Flavor Depth:** The combination of saffron, smoked paprika, and turmeric creates a depth of flavor in the rice that is rich and aromatic. Don't skimp on these spices—they're essential to the dish's authenticity.

- **Shellfish Variations:** Feel free to experiment with other shellfish like lobster or scallops. The shellfish can also be substituted with chicken or chorizo if you prefer a meat-based paella.

- **Perfect Rice Texture:** Black rice is naturally a bit more chewy than traditional white rice, but it pairs perfectly with the tender shellfish. Make sure not to overcook the rice; it should still have a slight bite when done.

Spanish-Style Steak Frites with Cabrales Blue Cheese

This dish takes inspiration from the French classic steak frites but adds a Spanish flair with the addition of Cabrales blue cheese. The creamy, tangy flavor of Cabrales perfectly complements the richness of the steak, while the crispy fries bring the perfect crunch.

Ingredients:

- **For the Steak:**
    - 2 rib-eye steaks, about 1 inch thick
    - 1 tablespoon olive oil
    - 1 tablespoon butter
    - 2 cloves garlic, smashed
    - 1 sprig rosemary
    - Salt and freshly ground black pepper to taste

- **For the Frites:**
    - 4 large russet potatoes, peeled and cut into thin fries
    - Vegetable oil for frying

- o Salt to taste
- **For the Cabrales Blue Cheese Sauce:**
    - o 1/2 cup heavy cream
    - o 1/4 cup Cabrales blue cheese, crumbled
    - o 1 tablespoon white vinegar vinegar
    - o Salt and freshly ground black pepper to taste

Preparation:

1. **Making the Frites:**
    - o Fill a large pot with vegetable oil and heat to 375°F. Working in batches, fry the potatoes until golden brown and crispy, about 4-5 minutes. Remove the fries from the oil and drain on paper towels. Season with salt immediately.

2. **Cooking the Steaks:**
    - o Preheat a cast-iron skillet over medium-high heat. Season the steaks with salt and pepper. Add olive oil and butter to the skillet, then add the steaks. Cook for 4-5 minutes per side for medium-rare, or adjust the cooking time based on your preference.
    - o Add the smashed garlic and rosemary sprig to the pan during the last minute of cooking, basting the steaks with the pan juices.

3. **Making the Cabrales Blue Cheese Sauce:**
    - o In a small saucepan, heat the heavy cream over medium heat. Once it begins to simmer, add the Cabrales blue cheese and stir until the cheese is melted and the sauce is smooth.
    - o Stir in the white vinegar vinegar and season with salt and pepper. Remove from heat.

4. **Assembling the Dish:**

- Place the cooked steaks on a serving plate. Pour the Cabrales blue cheese sauce over the top of the steaks, allowing the sauce to drape over the meat. Serve the crispy fries on the side.

Tips & Tricks:

- **Steak Doneness:** Use a meat thermometer to check the internal temperature of the steak for perfect doneness—130°F for medium-rare, 140°F for medium.

- **Fries Texture:** Double-frying the potatoes results in fries that are extra crispy. The first fry cooks the potatoes through, while the second fry crisps the outside.

- **Substitute Cheese:** If you can't find Cabrales blue cheese, Roquefort or Gorgonzola make excellent substitutes with similar tangy and creamy profiles.

Smoked Paprika Fries with Rioja Red Vinegar Sauce

Smoked paprika fries offer a smoky, savory twist on classic French fries, while the Rioja red vinegar sauce adds a rich, deep flavor that elevates the dish to something extraordinary. This recipe embodies Bobby Flay's ability to transform simple ingredients into something memorable.

Ingredients:

- **For the Fries:**
  - 4 large russet potatoes, peeled and cut into thin fries
  - 2 tablespoons smoked paprika
  - Vegetable oil for frying
  - Salt to taste

- **For the Rioja Red Vinegar Sauce:**

- 1/2 cup Rioja red vinegar
- 1/2 cup beef stock
- 1 tablespoon butter
- 1 small shallot, minced
- 1 sprig thyme
- Salt and freshly ground black pepper to taste

Preparation:

1. **Making the Fries:**
   - Fill a large pot with vegetable oil and heat to 375°F. Fry the potatoes in batches until golden brown and crispy. Drain on paper towels and season with smoked paprika and salt immediately.

2. **Making the Rioja Red Vinegar Sauce:**
   - In a small saucepan, melt butter over medium heat. Add the minced shallot and cook until soft, about 3-4 minutes. Add the Rioja vinegar and thyme, cooking for 5-7 minutes until the vinegar reduces by half.
   - Add the beef stock and continue to simmer until the sauce thickens, about 10 minutes. Season with salt and pepper to taste.

3. **Serving the Fries:**
   - Serve the crispy smoked paprika fries with the Rioja red vinegar sauce for dipping.

Tips & Tricks:

- **Vinegar Substitution:** If you don't have Rioja, a good Cabernet Sauvignon or Merlot can be used to make the sauce.
- **Crispy Fries:** Soaking the potatoes in cold water for 30 minutes before frying helps remove excess starch and results in extra crispy fries.

- **Herb Variations:** Experiment with adding different herbs to the red vinegar sauce, such as rosemary or sage, to customize the flavor.

Grilled Herb-Crusted Rack of Lamb

A tender, flavorful rack of lamb crusted with fresh herbs and garlic is a standout dish for any special occasion. Bobby Flay's herb-crusted rack of lamb is grilled to perfection, creating a beautiful balance of char and tenderness, with a rich, aromatic herb crust that elevates the dish.

Ingredients:

- 1 rack of lamb, frenched
- 2 tablespoons olive oil
- 2 tablespoons fresh rosemary, finely chopped
- 2 tablespoons fresh thyme, finely chopped
- 3 cloves garlic, minced
- 1 tablespoon Dijon mustard
- Salt and freshly ground black pepper to taste

Preparation:

1. **Preparing the Lamb:**
   - Preheat the grill to medium-high heat. Rub the rack of lamb with olive oil, then season with salt and pepper.
   - In a small bowl, combine the rosemary, thyme, garlic, and Dijon mustard. Rub the herb mixture evenly over the rack of lamb.

2. **Grilling the Lamb:**
   - Grill the lamb for 4-5 minutes per side for medium-rare, or adjust the time depending on your desired doneness. Use a meat

thermometer to check the internal temperature—130°F for medium-rare, 140°F for medium.

- Let the lamb rest for 5 minutes before slicing.

Tips & Tricks:

- **Herb Crust:** Fresh herbs are essential for a fragrant, flavorful crust. If fresh herbs aren't available, you can substitute with dried herbs, but reduce the quantity by half.

- **Grill Marks:** For perfect grill marks, make sure your grill is hot before adding the lamb, and rotate the rack halfway through cooking.

- **Resting the Meat:** Always let the lamb rest for a few minutes after grilling to allow the juices to redistribute for a tender, juicy result.

Buttermilk Fried Chicken with Honey-Hot Sauce

Fried chicken is a beloved American classic, and Bobby Flay's buttermilk fried chicken takes it to the next level with a crispy exterior, tender meat, and a sweet and spicy honey-hot sauce that adds a kick of flavor.

Ingredients:

- **For the Chicken:**
  - 4 chicken thighs, bone-in and skin-on
  - 1 cup buttermilk
  - 1 tablespoon hot sauce
  - 1 cup all-purpose flour
  - 1 teaspoon paprika
  - 1 teaspoon garlic powder
  - Salt and freshly ground black pepper to taste

- o Vegetable oil for frying
- **For the Honey-Hot Sauce:**
  - o 1/4 cup honey
  - o 2 tablespoons hot sauce
  - o 1 tablespoon apple cider vinegar
  - o Salt and pepper to taste

Preparation:

1. **Marinating the Chicken:**
   - o Combine buttermilk and hot sauce in a large bowl. Add the chicken thighs and let them marinate in the refrigerator for at least 2 hours or overnight.

2. **Frying the Chicken:**
   - o In a shallow dish, combine flour, paprika, garlic powder, salt, and pepper. Dredge the marinated chicken in the flour mixture, pressing gently to coat evenly.
   - o Heat vegetable oil in a large skillet over medium-high heat. Fry the chicken for 8-10 minutes per side, or until golden brown and cooked through. Use a meat thermometer to check the internal temperature—165°F for fully cooked chicken.

3. **Making the Honey-Hot Sauce:**
   - o In a small saucepan, combine honey, hot sauce, and apple cider vinegar. Bring to a simmer over medium heat, cooking for 3-4 minutes. Season with salt and pepper to taste.

4. **Serving the Chicken:**
   - o Drizzle the honey-hot sauce over the crispy fried chicken just before serving.

Tips & Tricks:

- **Fried Chicken Crunch:** Double-dipping the chicken (once in buttermilk and once in flour) helps create an extra-crunchy crust.

- **Spice Control:** Adjust the amount of hot sauce in both the marinade and the sauce to control the spice level of the dish.

- **Frying Temperature:** Use a thermometer to maintain the oil at 350°F to prevent the chicken from becoming greasy.

These dishes represent the bold, innovative spirit that Bobby Flay brings to modern American cuisine. Each recipe is a reflection of his culinary philosophy—combining traditional techniques with creative twists to produce a dining experience that is both familiar and exciting. By experimenting with new ingredients and bold flavors, Flay's New American classics continue to inspire home cooks and professional chefs alike.

Chapter 4: Flay's Signature Dishes

Introduction: Dishes That Define the Chef

Bobby Flay is a chef whose culinary style transcends trends. Known for his bold, creative approach, his signature dishes are the epitome of what defines him as a chef—distinctive, flavor-packed, and unmistakably his own. These are the dishes that have become synonymous with Flay's name and cooking philosophy: a perfect balance of heat, freshness, and irresistible textures. They reflect his mastery of combining bold flavors, technique, and a passion for ingredients that tell a story of authenticity and innovation.

Flay's signature dishes are the foundation of his identity in the culinary world. They represent his commitment to simplicity with flair, his love for using the best ingredients, and his dedication to creating unforgettable dining experiences. From smoky BBQ short ribs to fresh shrimp and chorizo tacos, each of these recipes reflects his ability to take familiar ingredients and transform them into something extraordinary.

Through these signature dishes, Bobby Flay invites you to experience the bold flavors of American cuisine with an international twist. Whether you are grilling, roasting, or making a quick meal on a busy weeknight, these recipes offer something for every occasion. In this chapter, we will delve into the essence of Bobby Flay's cooking style, showcasing the bold flavors and techniques that have made his signature dishes unforgettable.

BBQ Short Ribs with Roasted Garlic Mashed Potatoes

A true classic, Bobby Flay's BBQ short ribs have become one of the defining dishes of his culinary repertoire. With tender, fall-off-the-bone meat, smoky and sweet flavors, and a rich, flavorful sauce, this dish is perfect for gatherings or a hearty family dinner. The roasted garlic mashed potatoes add a creamy, flavorful complement to the richness of the ribs.

Ingredients:

- **For the Short Ribs:**
  - 4 beef short ribs, bone-in
  - 2 tablespoons olive oil
  - Salt and freshly ground black pepper to taste
  - 1/2 cup BBQ sauce (store-bought or homemade)
  - 2 cups beef stock
  - 1 tablespoon Dijon mustard
  - 2 tablespoons apple cider vinegar
  - 1/2 teaspoon smoked paprika
  - 1/4 teaspoon ground cumin
  - 1 tablespoon brown sugar
- **For the Roasted Garlic Mashed Potatoes:**
  - 2 pounds Yukon gold potatoes, peeled and cut into chunks
  - 1 bulb garlic
  - 4 tablespoons unsalted butter
  - 1/2 cup heavy cream
  - Salt and freshly ground black pepper to taste
  - Fresh chives for garnish

Preparation:

1. **Roasting the Garlic:**
   - Preheat the oven to 400°F. Slice the top off the garlic bulb, exposing the individual cloves. Drizzle with olive oil, wrap in foil, and roast for about 30-40 minutes, until the garlic is soft and golden. Once cool enough to handle, squeeze the garlic cloves out of their skins and set aside.

2. **Preparing the Short Ribs:**

   o Season the short ribs generously with salt and pepper. Heat olive oil in a large oven-safe Dutch oven or heavy pot over medium-high heat. Brown the short ribs on all sides, about 5-6 minutes total.

   o Once browned, remove the short ribs and set aside. Add the BBQ sauce, beef stock, Dijon mustard, apple cider vinegar, smoked paprika, cumin, and brown sugar to the pot, stirring to combine.

   o Return the short ribs to the pot, making sure they're partially submerged in the liquid. Cover the pot with a lid and place in the oven. Roast at 325°F for 2.5 to 3 hours, or until the meat is tender and falling off the bone.

3. **Making the Mashed Potatoes:**

   o While the ribs are cooking, bring a large pot of salted water to a boil. Add the potatoes and cook until tender, about 15-20 minutes.

   o Drain the potatoes and return them to the pot. Add the roasted garlic cloves, butter, and heavy cream. Mash until smooth, adding salt and pepper to taste. Keep warm.

4. **Serving:**

   o When the ribs are ready, remove them from the pot and serve on a platter. Spoon some of the braising liquid over the top of the ribs. Serve the BBQ short ribs alongside the roasted garlic mashed potatoes, garnished with fresh chives.

Tips & Tricks:

- **Get Extra Flavor:** For extra smoky flavor, you can grill the short ribs before braising them. This will give the meat a rich, grilled flavor that complements the BBQ sauce.

- **Make-Ahead:** This dish is perfect for making ahead. The short ribs can be cooked the day before and reheated in the sauce, which will allow the flavors to meld even further.

- **Mashed Potato Perfection:** Yukon gold potatoes make the creamiest mashed potatoes, but russet potatoes work well too. If you want ultra-smooth potatoes, use a potato ricer instead of a masher.

Signature Burger with Jalapeño, Smoked Cheddar, and Chipotle Mayo

Flay's signature burger is a bold and juicy creation that takes the traditional burger to new heights. The combination of smoky cheddar, spicy jalapeños, and creamy chipotle mayo creates a flavor explosion that pairs perfectly with a perfectly grilled beef patty. This burger has become a favorite of fans and has helped redefine what a great burger should be.

Ingredients:

- **For the Burger:**
    - 1 pound ground chuck (80% lean)
    - Salt and freshly ground black pepper to taste
    - 4 hamburger buns, lightly toasted
    - 1 jalapeño, sliced
    - 4 slices smoked cheddar cheese
    - Lettuce, for garnish
    - Tomato slices, for garnish
- **For the Chipotle Mayo:**
    - 1/2 cup mayonnaise
    - 1-2 chipotle peppers in adobo sauce, finely chopped
    - 1 tablespoon adobo sauce
    - 1 tablespoon fresh lime juice
    - Salt to taste

Preparation:

1. **Making the Chipotle Mayo:**

   o In a small bowl, combine mayonnaise, chopped chipotle peppers, adobo sauce, and lime juice. Stir until smooth. Season with salt to taste. Set aside.

2. **Preparing the Burgers:**

   o Preheat the grill to medium-high heat. Season the ground beef with salt and pepper, then divide it into 4 equal portions. Form the portions into patties that are slightly larger than the buns.

   o Grill the patties for about 4-5 minutes per side for medium doneness, or longer if you prefer your burger cooked more.

   o During the last minute of grilling, place a slice of smoked cheddar on each patty to melt.

3. **Assembling the Burger:**

   o Spread a generous amount of chipotle mayo on the bottom bun. Add the lettuce, then place the grilled burger patty on top. Add the sliced jalapeños, tomato, and the top bun.

   o Serve immediately, accompanied by fries or your favorite side.

Tips & Tricks:

- **Burger Juiciness:** When forming the burger patties, avoid pressing down on the patties while grilling. This will help the burgers retain their juices and remain tender.

- **Customize the Heat:** If you like a milder flavor, you can reduce the amount of chipotle peppers in the mayo or remove the seeds from the jalapeños.

- **Grilled Veggies:** Consider adding grilled onions or mushrooms for extra flavor and texture.

Salt-Crusted Tuna with Roasted Beet Salad

A stunning and refined dish, Bobby Flay's salt-crusted tuna is as impressive as it is delicious. The salt crust helps to seal in the moisture and intensify the natural flavors of the tuna. Paired with a vibrant roasted beet salad, this dish feels luxurious while being surprisingly easy to prepare.

Ingredients:

- **For the Salt-Crusted Tuna:**
    - 2 tuna steaks, about 1 inch thick
    - 2 cups coarse sea salt
    - 1 tablespoon olive oil
    - Freshly ground black pepper to taste
- **For the Roasted Beet Salad:**
    - 4 small beets, peeled and cut into wedges
    - 1 tablespoon olive oil
    - Salt and pepper to taste
    - 1/4 cup goat cheese, crumbled
    - 1/4 cup toasted walnuts
    - Fresh arugula, for garnish
    - 1 tablespoon balsamic vinegar

Preparation:

1. **Roasting the Beets:**
    - Preheat the oven to 375°F. Toss the beet wedges in olive oil, salt, and pepper. Roast in a single layer on a baking sheet for about 25-30 minutes, or until tender. Let cool.

2. **Preparing the Tuna:**

   o Preheat the oven to 450°F. Coat the tuna steaks with olive oil, salt, and pepper. Roll the tuna steaks in the coarse sea salt, pressing gently to coat.

   o Heat a nonstick skillet over medium-high heat. Sear the tuna steaks for about 2 minutes on each side for a rare to medium-rare result.

   o Transfer the tuna steaks to the oven and bake for 5-7 minutes, depending on your desired doneness.

3. **Making the Salad:**

   o In a bowl, toss the roasted beets with arugula, crumbled goat cheese, and toasted walnuts. Drizzle with balsamic vinegar and season with salt and pepper.

4. **Serving:**

   o Slice the salt-crusted tuna and arrange it on a plate. Serve alongside the roasted beet salad.

Tips & Tricks:

- **Perfect Tuna:** Salt-crusting the tuna creates a delicate, slightly salty exterior while keeping the inside tender and juicy. If you prefer a more pronounced crust, you can leave the tuna in the salt crust for an extra minute or two.

- **Beet Variations:** If you prefer a milder beet flavor, try roasting the beets with orange slices for an added citrus touch.

- **Walnut Substitute:** For a different flavor, you can substitute the walnuts with toasted pecans or hazelnuts.

Shrimp and Chorizo Tacos with Cilantro-Lime Slaw

This dish combines the smoky heat of chorizo with the sweetness of shrimp for a dynamic taco filling. Topped with a tangy cilantro-lime slaw, these tacos burst with flavor and freshness, making them a popular choice for casual meals and gatherings.

Ingredients:

- **For the Shrimp and Chorizo:**
    - 1/2 pound shrimp, peeled and deveined
    - 1/2 pound chorizo, casing removed
    - 1 tablespoon olive oil
    - Salt and freshly ground black pepper to taste
    - 8 small corn tortillas
- **For the Cilantro-Lime Slaw:**
    - 2 cups shredded cabbage
    - 1/4 cup chopped fresh cilantro
    - 2 tablespoons lime juice
    - 1 tablespoon mayonnaise
    - 1 teaspoon sugar
    - Salt and pepper to taste

Preparation:

1. **Preparing the Shrimp and Chorizo:**
    - Heat olive oil in a large skillet over medium heat. Add the chorizo and cook, breaking it up with a spoon, for about 5 minutes, until browned and crispy.

o Add the shrimp to the skillet with the chorizo and cook for an additional 2-3 minutes, until the shrimp turn pink and opaque.

2. **Making the Slaw:**

   o In a large bowl, combine shredded cabbage, cilantro, lime juice, mayonnaise, sugar, salt, and pepper. Toss to combine.

3. **Assembling the Tacos:**

   o Warm the corn tortillas in a skillet or microwave. Spoon the shrimp and chorizo mixture onto each tortilla and top with the cilantro-lime slaw.

   o Serve with lime wedges for extra tang.

Tips & Tricks:

- **Taco Variations:** If you want a spicier kick, add a few slices of jalapeño to the slaw or garnish the tacos with a spicy salsa.

- **Tortilla Options:** For a healthier alternative, you can use lettuce wraps instead of tortillas.

- **Shrimp Cooking:** Don't overcook the shrimp—just cook until they turn pink to keep them juicy and tender.

Roasted Salmon with Lemon-Caper Sauce and Garlic Spinach

This recipe brings together the richness of roasted salmon with the brightness of a lemon-caper sauce and the earthiness of sautéed garlic spinach. It's a light but flavorful dish that can be served as part of a weeknight dinner or a special meal for guests.

Ingredients:

- **For the Roasted Salmon:**

- o 4 salmon fillets
- o 2 tablespoons olive oil
- o Salt and pepper to taste
- **For the Lemon-Caper Sauce:**
  - o 1/4 cup lemon juice
  - o 2 tablespoons capers, drained and chopped
  - o 1 tablespoon butter
  - o Freshly ground black pepper to taste
- **For the Garlic Spinach:**
  - o 1 pound fresh spinach
  - o 2 cloves garlic, minced
  - o 1 tablespoon olive oil
  - o Salt and pepper to taste

Preparation:

1. **Roasting the Salmon:**
   - o Preheat the oven to 400°F. Place the salmon fillets on a baking sheet lined with parchment paper. Drizzle with olive oil and season with salt and pepper. Roast for 10-12 minutes or until the salmon is cooked through.

2. **Making the Lemon-Caper Sauce:**
   - o In a small saucepan, combine lemon juice and capers. Bring to a simmer and cook for 2-3 minutes. Stir in butter until melted and smooth. Season with pepper.

3. **Making the Garlic Spinach:**

- Heat olive oil in a large skillet over medium heat. Add the garlic and cook for 1 minute until fragrant. Add the spinach and cook, stirring, until wilted. Season with salt and pepper.

4. **Serving:**

- Plate the roasted salmon fillets and spoon the lemon-caper sauce over the top. Serve with garlic spinach on the side.

Tips & Tricks:

- **Perfect Salmon:** To check for doneness, gently press the salmon with a fork—if it flakes easily, it's done.

- **Spinach Variations:** Add a sprinkle of red pepper flakes or a squeeze of fresh lemon juice to the spinach for extra flavor.

- **Make Ahead:** The lemon-caper sauce can be made ahead of time and stored in the fridge for up to 3 days.

Through these signature dishes, Bobby Flay demonstrates the importance of layering flavors and focusing on ingredients that bring a sense of place and purpose to each dish. Each recipe in this chapter not only showcases his skill and creativity but also offers an opportunity for home cooks to create memorable meals that reflect Flay's culinary philosophy.

Chapter 5: Mediterranean Influences

Introduction: Bringing the Flavors of the Mediterranean to America

The Mediterranean diet, celebrated for its balance, simplicity, and vibrant flavors, has been one of the most influential culinary traditions worldwide. Bobby Flay, known for his diverse and adventurous approach to cuisine, has long been inspired by Mediterranean cooking. His interpretation of these dishes brings together the freshest ingredients, bold herbs, and spices, with an innovative twist that resonates with the American palate. The flavors of the Mediterranean—rich in olive oils, fresh vegetables, fish, and grilled meats— meld perfectly with Flay's love for grilling, smoky aromas, and bold seasonings.

This chapter explores how Flay infuses Mediterranean influences into his own cooking style. His recipes marry the fresh, simple, and healthful ingredients of the Mediterranean region with his signature flair, bringing vibrant new dishes to American tables. From grilled octopus to savory lamb chops, each dish offers a taste of the Mediterranean, seasoned with Flay's unique creative edge. Whether grilling or slow-cooking, these recipes embrace Mediterranean traditions, but with a distinct modern twist.

Through these Mediterranean-inspired dishes, you'll find new ways to enjoy some of the region's most iconic flavors, all while keeping your meals fresh, exciting, and full of flavor. Here, we explore how Bobby Flay's culinary approach transforms these traditional Mediterranean dishes, making them accessible to anyone looking to explore this vibrant cuisine.

Grilled Mediterranean Octopus with Olive Tapenade

Octopus is a star ingredient in Mediterranean cuisine, particularly in countries like Greece, Spain, and Italy. It's prized for its tender texture and ability to absorb deep flavors. Flay's grilled Mediterranean octopus takes this tender seafood and brings out its smoky, savory flavors by grilling it to perfection and pairing it with a rich, briny olive tapenade.

Ingredients:

- **For the Octopus:**
  - 2 pounds octopus, cleaned
  - 1/4 cup olive oil
  - 2 cloves garlic, minced
  - 1 lemon, zested and juiced
  - 1 tablespoon fresh oregano, finely chopped
  - Salt and freshly ground black pepper to taste
- **For the Olive Tapenade:**
  - 1 cup Kalamata olives, pitted
  - 1/2 cup green olives, pitted
  - 2 tablespoons capers, drained
  - 2 cloves garlic, minced
  - 1 tablespoon lemon juice
  - 1/4 cup extra-virgin olive oil
  - Fresh parsley, chopped, for garnish

Preparation:

1. **Preparing the Octopus:**
   - Start by tenderizing the octopus. This can be done by either boiling it for about 45 minutes in a large pot of water until tender or using a meat mallet to gently pound the flesh to soften it. Once tender, cut the octopus into 3-inch pieces, keeping the tentacles intact.

- o In a bowl, combine olive oil, minced garlic, lemon zest, fresh oregano, salt, and pepper. Toss the octopus pieces in this marinade and refrigerate for at least 1 hour, allowing the flavors to infuse.

2. **Making the Olive Tapenade:**

- o In a food processor, pulse together Kalamata olives, green olives, capers, garlic, and lemon juice until coarsely chopped. With the motor running, slowly drizzle in the olive oil until the tapenade becomes a chunky paste. Adjust the seasoning with salt and pepper to taste. Set aside.

3. **Grilling the Octopus:**

- o Preheat a grill or grill pan to medium-high heat. Grill the octopus pieces for 2-3 minutes per side, or until slightly charred and crispy on the outside, while still tender inside.

4. **Serving:**

- o Serve the grilled octopus on a platter, topped with a spoonful of olive tapenade. Garnish with freshly chopped parsley and an extra drizzle of olive oil if desired.

Tips & Tricks:

- **Tenderizing Octopus:** If boiling the octopus, be sure not to overcook it. Test for tenderness by inserting a fork into the thickest part of a tentacle—if it's tender and easily pulls apart, it's done.

- **Marinating Time:** Marinating the octopus for at least an hour gives it the chance to absorb the garlic, lemon, and oregano, but don't marinate for too long, as the acidity from the lemon can start to break down the meat.

- **Tapenade Variations:** You can customize the tapenade by adding anchovies or roasted red peppers for additional depth of flavor.

Chicken Shawarma with Pita and Hummus

Shawarma is a popular street food in the Middle East, known for its aromatic spices, tender meat, and irresistible flavor. Bobby Flay's version of chicken shawarma brings the same delicious experience, offering a grilled chicken that's perfectly spiced and served with warm pita and creamy hummus. This dish captures the essence of Mediterranean street food while providing a more elevated and refined version that you can easily prepare at home.

Ingredients:

- **For the Chicken Marinade:**
  - 4 boneless, skinless chicken thighs
  - 3 tablespoons olive oil
  - 2 tablespoons lemon juice
  - 3 cloves garlic, minced
  - 1 tablespoon ground cumin
  - 1 tablespoon ground coriander
  - 1 tablespoon paprika
  - 1/2 teaspoon ground turmeric
  - 1/4 teaspoon ground cinnamon
  - Salt and freshly ground black pepper to taste
- **For the Hummus:**
  - 1 can (15 ounces) chickpeas, drained and rinsed
  - 1/4 cup tahini
  - 2 tablespoons lemon juice
  - 1 tablespoon olive oil
  - 1 clove garlic, minced
  - Salt to taste

- Water, as needed to adjust consistency
- **To Serve:**
    - 4 pita breads, warmed
    - Fresh cilantro, chopped
    - Pickled vegetables (optional)

Preparation:

1. **Marinating the Chicken:**
    - In a large bowl, combine olive oil, lemon juice, garlic, cumin, coriander, paprika, turmeric, cinnamon, salt, and pepper. Add the chicken thighs and coat well. Cover and refrigerate for at least 2 hours, or up to overnight, allowing the flavors to penetrate the meat.

2. **Making the Hummus:**
    - In a food processor, combine chickpeas, tahini, lemon juice, olive oil, garlic, and a pinch of salt. Process until smooth. If the mixture is too thick, add water, one tablespoon at a time, until the hummus reaches your desired consistency.

3. **Grilling the Chicken:**
    - Preheat a grill or grill pan to medium-high heat. Grill the chicken thighs for about 5-6 minutes per side, or until fully cooked and charred. The internal temperature should reach 165°F. Let the chicken rest for 5 minutes before slicing thinly.

4. **Serving:**
    - Serve the sliced shawarma chicken on warm pita bread. Add a generous dollop of hummus, top with fresh cilantro, and serve with pickled vegetables on the side if desired.

Tips & Tricks:

- **Tenderizing Chicken:** Chicken thighs are ideal for shawarma as they remain juicy and tender when grilled. However, you can use chicken breasts if you prefer. Just be mindful not to overcook them, as they tend to dry out faster.

- **Hummus Texture:** For smoother hummus, peel the skins off the chickpeas before blending. This can be a little time-consuming but results in a silky-smooth dip.

- **Serving Ideas:** Add a side of tabbouleh or a cucumber and tomato salad to complete the meal.

Charred Vegetables with Tzatziki Sauce

Grilled vegetables are a cornerstone of Mediterranean cooking, and they're often paired with a tangy, refreshing tzatziki sauce. Flay's charred vegetables offer a smoky, rich flavor that contrasts beautifully with the cool and creamy tzatziki, making this dish a perfect side or light main course.

Ingredients:

- **For the Vegetables:**
  - 2 zucchini, sliced lengthwise
  - 2 bell peppers, cut into large chunks
  - 1 red onion, cut into wedges
  - 1/2 eggplant, sliced into rounds
  - 1 tablespoon olive oil
  - Salt and freshly ground black pepper to taste

- **For the Tzatziki Sauce:**
  - 1 cup Greek yogurt
  - 1/2 cucumber, grated and excess moisture squeezed out
  - 2 cloves garlic, minced

- 1 tablespoon fresh dill, chopped
- 1 tablespoon fresh lemon juice
- Salt and pepper to taste

Preparation:

1. **Grilling the Vegetables:**
   - Preheat a grill or grill pan to medium-high heat. Toss the vegetables with olive oil, salt, and pepper. Grill the vegetables for about 3-4 minutes per side until charred and tender, being careful not to overcook.

2. **Making the Tzatziki Sauce:**
   - In a bowl, combine Greek yogurt, grated cucumber, garlic, dill, and lemon juice. Stir well and season with salt and pepper. Chill in the fridge until ready to serve.

3. **Serving:**
   - Arrange the grilled vegetables on a platter and serve with a generous drizzle of tzatziki sauce. Garnish with additional fresh dill and a squeeze of lemon.

Tips & Tricks:

- **Vegetable Variations:** You can add other vegetables like cherry tomatoes or asparagus, depending on what's in season.

- **Tzatziki Tips:** If you prefer a stronger garlic flavor, add an extra clove of garlic to the tzatziki sauce.

- **Grilling Vegetables:** Be sure not to overcrowd the grill, as this can cause the vegetables to steam rather than char. If needed, grill in batches.

Lobster and Tomato Ragout with Saffron Risotto

This dish showcases the luxurious flavors of lobster paired with a fragrant saffron risotto. The ragout, with its rich, garlicky tomato sauce, complements the lobster, creating a dish that is both comforting and refined. The addition of saffron in the risotto adds an aromatic, slightly floral note that enhances the seafood's natural sweetness.

Ingredients:

- **For the Lobster Ragout:**
    - 2 lobster tails, shelled and cut into chunks
    - 2 tablespoons olive oil
    - 2 cloves garlic, minced
    - 1 can (14.5 ounces) diced tomatoes
    - 1/4 cup white vinegar
    - 1 tablespoon fresh basil, chopped
    - Salt and pepper to taste

- **For the Saffron Risotto:**
    - 1 tablespoon olive oil
    - 1 small onion, finely chopped
    - 1 cup Arborio rice
    - 1/4 teaspoon saffron threads
    - 4 cups chicken or vegetable stock, kept warm
    - 1/2 cup dry white vinegar
    - 1/4 cup grated Parmesan cheese
    - Salt and pepper to taste

Preparation:

1. **Making the Lobster Ragout:**
   - ○ Heat olive oil in a large skillet over medium heat. Add garlic and cook for 1-2 minutes until fragrant. Add the diced tomatoes and white vinegar, simmering for about 10 minutes to allow the sauce to reduce. Add the lobster chunks and cook for an additional 3-4 minutes until the lobster is cooked through. Stir in fresh basil and season with salt and pepper.

2. **Making the Saffron Risotto:**
   - ○ In a saucepan, heat olive oil and sauté onion for 2-3 minutes until soft. Add Arborio rice and cook, stirring, for 2 minutes. Add saffron threads and a ladle of warm stock, stirring constantly. Continue adding stock, one ladle at a time, stirring constantly, until the rice is tender and creamy (about 20 minutes). Stir in Parmesan cheese and season with salt and pepper.

3. **Serving:**
   - ○ Serve the lobster ragout over a bed of saffron risotto, garnished with fresh basil and a drizzle of olive oil.

Tips & Tricks:

- **Lobster Tips:** Don't overcook the lobster! It only takes 3-4 minutes to cook through, and overcooking can result in rubbery meat.

- **Risotto Consistency:** Keep the stock warm to prevent the cooking process from slowing down. Stirring continuously releases the starch in the rice, giving the risotto its creamy texture.

- **Vinegar Pairing:** Pair this dish with a crisp white vinegar, such as a Sauvignon Blanc or Chardonnay.

Grilled Lamb Chops with Mint Yogurt Sauce

Lamb is a beloved protein in Mediterranean cooking, prized for its tender, flavorful meat. Bobby Flay's grilled lamb chops, paired with a refreshing mint yogurt sauce, are an iconic dish that highlights the bold flavors of the Mediterranean. The smoky char from the grill complements the rich lamb, while the cool yogurt sauce provides a refreshing contrast.

Ingredients:

- **For the Lamb Chops:**
    - 8 lamb chops
    - 3 tablespoons olive oil
    - 2 tablespoons fresh rosemary, chopped
    - 2 cloves garlic, minced
    - Salt and freshly ground black pepper to taste

- **For the Mint Yogurt Sauce:**
    - 1 cup Greek yogurt
    - 1/4 cup fresh mint, chopped
    - 1 tablespoon lemon juice
    - Salt and pepper to taste

Preparation:

1. **Marinating the Lamb:**
    - In a bowl, combine olive oil, rosemary, garlic, salt, and pepper. Coat the lamb chops with the marinade and refrigerate for at least 30 minutes, or up to overnight.

2. **Making the Mint Yogurt Sauce:**
    - In a bowl, combine Greek yogurt, chopped mint, lemon juice, salt, and pepper. Stir well and chill in the fridge until ready to serve.

3. **Grilling the Lamb:**

   o Preheat the grill to medium-high heat. Grill the lamb chops for about 4-5 minutes per side for medium-rare, or longer if you prefer them more well-done. Let the lamb rest for a few minutes before serving.

4. **Serving:**

   o Serve the grilled lamb chops with a generous drizzle of mint yogurt sauce on the side.

Tips & Tricks:

- **Lamb Cooking Tips:** Use a meat thermometer to check the internal temperature of the lamb chops. For medium-rare, aim for 135°F, and for medium, 145°F.

- **Mint Yogurt Sauce:** Add a touch of honey to the mint yogurt sauce if you prefer a slightly sweet contrast to the lamb.

- **Grill Marks:** Ensure your grill is preheated before placing the lamb chops on it, as this will help create those perfect grill marks.

These Mediterranean-inspired dishes showcase Bobby Flay's ability to bring bold, fresh flavors into the American kitchen. His take on Mediterranean classics offers a perfect balance of tradition and innovation, and each recipe brings the vibrant, sunny flavors of the Mediterranean into your home.

Chapter 6: Comfort Food Reinvented

Introduction: Elevating the Classics

Comfort food is the heart and soul of American cuisine, often evoking feelings of nostalgia, warmth, and satisfaction. These are the dishes that remind us of family gatherings, childhood memories, and the simple joys of home-cooked meals. While comfort food is inherently humble and unpretentious, it is also an area where chefs have the opportunity to experiment, elevate, and reimagine what it can be. Bobby Flay, known for his bold flavors and inventive approach to cooking, has taken the concept of comfort food and turned it on its head.

In this chapter, we explore how Bobby Flay's signature twists on classic comfort foods bring new layers of flavor, texture, and complexity. Each recipe retains the essence of the original dish but is enhanced with ingredients and techniques that elevate it to something truly special. From rich and creamy mac and cheese with the luxury of truffle oil to a meatloaf with a spicy chipotle ketchup glaze, these reinvented comfort foods are designed to surprise and delight.

By adding a bit of sophistication, creativity, and of course, bold flavors, Flay brings an updated spin to comfort classics. Let's dive into the recipes that will transform your favorite nostalgic dishes into gourmet creations.

Mac & Cheese with Truffle Oil and Wild Mushrooms

Mac and cheese is the quintessential comfort food—rich, creamy, and cheesy. Bobby Flay takes this beloved dish and makes it truly luxurious by adding earthy wild mushrooms and the unmistakable flavor of truffle oil. The result is an elevated version of the classic, one that's perfect for both weeknight dinners and special occasions.

Ingredients:

- **For the Mac & Cheese:**
  - 1 pound elbow macaroni
  - 2 tablespoons unsalted butter
  - 2 tablespoons all-purpose flour
  - 4 cups whole milk
  - 2 cups heavy cream
  - 2 cups grated Gruyère cheese
  - 1 ½ cups grated sharp cheddar cheese
  - 1 cup wild mushrooms (such as shiitake, chanterelle, or cremini), sliced
  - 2 tablespoons truffle oil
  - Salt and freshly ground black pepper to taste
  - Fresh chives, chopped, for garnish
- **For the Topping:**
  - 1/2 cup panko breadcrumbs
  - 1 tablespoon unsalted butter, melted
  - 1/4 cup grated Parmesan cheese

Preparation:

1. **Cook the Pasta:**
   - Bring a large pot of salted water to a boil. Add the elbow macaroni and cook according to the package instructions until al dente. Drain and set aside.

2. **Make the Cheese Sauce:**
   - In a large saucepan, melt the butter over medium heat. Once melted, add the flour and cook, whisking constantly, for about 2 minutes to form a roux.

- Slowly add the milk and heavy cream to the roux, whisking constantly to avoid lumps. Bring the mixture to a simmer and cook until thickened, about 5 minutes.
- Stir in the Gruyère and cheddar cheeses until melted and smooth. Season with salt and freshly ground black pepper.

3. **Sauté the Mushrooms:**

- In a separate skillet, heat the truffle oil over medium heat. Add the wild mushrooms and sauté until tender and browned, about 4-5 minutes. Season with a pinch of salt and pepper.

4. **Combine the Pasta, Cheese Sauce, and Mushrooms:**

- Add the cooked macaroni to the cheese sauce and stir to combine. Fold in the sautéed mushrooms and mix gently.

5. **Prepare the Topping:**

- In a small bowl, combine the panko breadcrumbs, melted butter, and Parmesan cheese. Sprinkle the mixture over the top of the mac and cheese.

6. **Bake the Mac & Cheese:**

- Preheat the oven to 375°F (190°C). Transfer the mac and cheese to a greased 9x13-inch baking dish. Bake for 20 minutes, or until the top is golden and crispy.

7. **Garnish and Serve:**

- Drizzle a little extra truffle oil over the top and garnish with freshly chopped chives. Serve hot and enjoy the creamy, cheesy goodness with a touch of elegance.

Tips & Tricks:

- **Truffle Oil:** When using truffle oil, it's important to use it sparingly, as it can be quite potent. Just a drizzle is enough to impart a deep, earthy flavor to the dish.

- **Cheese Selection:** Gruyère adds a nutty, melty richness to the sauce, while sharp cheddar gives it a tangy bite. Feel free to experiment with other cheeses such as fontina or provolone for different flavor profiles.

- **Mushrooms:** Wild mushrooms provide an earthy flavor that complements the richness of the cheese. If wild mushrooms aren't available, cremini or button mushrooms can work just as well.

- **Make-Ahead:** This mac and cheese can be made ahead of time and refrigerated. Simply bake it when you're ready to serve, and it'll taste just as fresh and indulgent.

Sweet Potato Gratin with Parmesan and Garlic

Sweet potatoes are a versatile and nutritious vegetable that's often overlooked in comfort food. Flay's sweet potato gratin transforms this humble root vegetable into something luxurious. The thinly sliced sweet potatoes are layered with garlic, cream, and Parmesan cheese, creating a rich, savory dish with a slight sweetness from the potatoes that balances out the richness of the sauce.

Ingredients:

- 4 large sweet potatoes, peeled and thinly sliced
- 2 tablespoons unsalted butter
- 3 cloves garlic, minced
- 2 cups heavy cream
- 1 cup whole milk
- 1 ½ cups grated Parmesan cheese
- 2 teaspoons fresh thyme leaves
- Salt and freshly ground black pepper to taste
- 1/2 cup panko breadcrumbs

Preparation:

1. **Preheat the Oven:**

   o Preheat the oven to 375°F (190°C). Butter a 9x13-inch baking dish.

2. **Prepare the Cream Sauce:**

   o In a saucepan, melt the butter over medium heat. Add the minced garlic and sauté until fragrant, about 1 minute.

   o Add the heavy cream, milk, and thyme. Bring the mixture to a simmer and cook for 5 minutes. Season with salt and pepper to taste.

3. **Assemble the Gratin:**

   o Arrange a layer of thinly sliced sweet potatoes in the bottom of the prepared baking dish. Pour a portion of the cream mixture over the potatoes, then sprinkle with Parmesan cheese.

   o Repeat the process, layering the sweet potatoes and pouring the cream mixture over each layer until all the potatoes are used. Top with the remaining Parmesan cheese.

4. **Bake the Gratin:**

   o Cover the baking dish with foil and bake for 40 minutes. Remove the foil and bake for an additional 20 minutes, or until the potatoes are tender and the top is golden brown.

5. **Prepare the Topping:**

   o In a small bowl, toss the panko breadcrumbs with a tablespoon of melted butter. Sprinkle the breadcrumbs over the top of the gratin and bake for another 10 minutes, until golden and crispy.

6. **Serve:**

   o Let the gratin rest for a few minutes before serving. Enjoy the rich, creamy layers of sweet potato and cheese.

Tips & Tricks:

- **Thin Slicing:** For even cooking, be sure to slice the sweet potatoes as thinly as possible. A mandoline slicer is ideal for this task.

- **Cheese Substitution:** If you prefer a stronger flavor, try using Gruyère or aged cheddar in place of Parmesan. These cheeses will melt beautifully and add a deep flavor.

- **Make-Ahead:** This gratin can be assembled the day before and refrigerated. Simply bake it when you're ready to serve.

Crispy Potato Skins with Bacon, Cheddar, and Chive Sour Cream

Potato skins are a classic comfort food that's both hearty and indulgent. Flay takes this favorite appetizer and gives it a gourmet twist by stuffing the crispy potato skins with smoky bacon, sharp cheddar cheese, and a tangy chive sour cream. The combination of textures and flavors makes these potato skins a perfect dish for parties or as a side for any meal.

Ingredients:

- 4 large russet potatoes
- 2 tablespoons olive oil
- Salt and freshly ground black pepper
- 1/2 cup cooked bacon, crumbled
- 1 ½ cups shredded cheddar cheese
- 1/4 cup sour cream
- 2 tablespoons fresh chives, chopped
- 1 tablespoon fresh parsley, chopped

Preparation:

1. **Bake the Potatoes:**
   - Preheat the oven to 400°F (200°C). Rub the potatoes with olive oil and season with salt and pepper. Bake the potatoes directly on the oven rack for 45 minutes, or until tender.

2. **Prepare the Potato Skins:**
   - Let the potatoes cool slightly, then slice them in half lengthwise. Carefully scoop out most of the flesh, leaving a small border of potato around the skin. Save the scooped-out potato for mashed potatoes or another recipe.

3. **Crisp the Skins:**
   - Brush the inside of the potato skins with olive oil and season with salt and pepper. Place them on a baking sheet, skin-side down, and bake for an additional 10-15 minutes, until crispy and golden.

4. **Assemble the Skins:**
   - Fill the crispy potato skins with crumbled bacon and shredded cheddar cheese. Return to the oven and bake for 5-7 minutes, until the cheese is melted and bubbly.

5. **Prepare the Sour Cream Topping:**
   - In a small bowl, combine sour cream, chopped chives, and parsley. Season with salt and pepper.

6. **Serve:**
   - Remove the potato skins from the oven and top with a dollop of chive sour cream. Garnish with extra chives and parsley.

Tips & Tricks:

- **Crispy Skins:** Make sure the skins are completely dry before baking to ensure they get crispy. You can also brush them with butter for a richer flavor.

- **Bacon Tips:** For extra smoky flavor, try using thick-cut bacon and cooking it until extra crispy before crumbling it into the potato skins.

- **Make-Ahead:** You can prep the potato skins ahead of time and store them in the fridge until you're ready to bake them with the fillings.

Meatloaf with Chipotle Ketchup and Roasted Brussels Sprouts

Meatloaf is another classic comfort food that often brings back memories of family dinners. Bobby Flay takes this simple dish and elevates it with the smoky, spicy kick of chipotle ketchup and perfectly roasted Brussels sprouts. The meatloaf is tender and flavorful, with the rich ketchup glaze adding just the right amount of sweetness and heat.

Ingredients:

- **For the Meatloaf:**
  - 1 pound ground beef
  - 1/2 pound ground beef
  - 1 small onion, finely chopped
  - 2 cloves garlic, minced
  - 1/2 cup bread crumbs
  - 1/4 cup milk
  - 1 large egg
  - 1 tablespoon Worcestershire sauce
  - Salt and freshly ground black pepper to taste

- **For the Chipotle Ketchup:**
  - 1 cup ketchup
  - 2 tablespoons chipotle in adobo sauce, minced

- o 1 tablespoon honey
- o 1 tablespoon red vinegar vinegar
- o 1 teaspoon smoked paprika
- **For the Brussels Sprouts:**
  - o 1 pound Brussels sprouts, trimmed and halved
  - o 2 tablespoons olive oil
  - o Salt and freshly ground black pepper

Preparation:

1. **Prepare the Meatloaf:**
   - o Preheat the oven to 350°F (175°C). In a large bowl, combine the ground beef, ground beef, chopped onion, garlic, bread crumbs, milk, egg, Worcestershire sauce, salt, and pepper. Mix until just combined, being careful not to overwork the meat.

2. **Shape and Bake the Meatloaf:**
   - o Transfer the meat mixture into a loaf pan, pressing it into an even layer. Bake for 45-50 minutes, or until the internal temperature reaches 160°F (71°C).

3. **Make the Chipotle Ketchup:**
   - o In a small saucepan, combine the ketchup, chipotle, honey, red vinegar vinegar, and smoked paprika. Simmer over low heat for 10 minutes, until thickened. Season with salt to taste.

4. **Roast the Brussels Sprouts:**
   - o Toss the Brussels sprouts with olive oil, salt, and pepper. Roast them on a baking sheet for 20-25 minutes, or until crispy and caramelized.

5. **Serve:**

o Drizzle the chipotle ketchup over the meatloaf and serve with the roasted Brussels sprouts on the side.

Tips & Tricks:

- **Moist Meatloaf:** Don't overmix the meatloaf mixture, as this can make the loaf tough. Just mix until everything is combined.

- **Brussels Sprouts:** Be sure to cut the Brussels sprouts into even halves for uniform cooking. You can also add a squeeze of lemon juice after roasting for an extra burst of flavor.

- **Spicy Ketchup:** Adjust the amount of chipotle depending on your spice preference. For a milder version, use less chipotle or remove the seeds before mincing.

Flay's Ultimate Macaroni Salad

Macaroni salad is a classic side dish often served at barbecues, picnics, and family gatherings. Bobby Flay's version adds a bit of flair with a tangy mustard dressing, sweet pickles, and a touch of fresh herbs. It's the perfect side to balance out rich, grilled meats or fried chicken.

Ingredients:

- 1 pound elbow macaroni
- 1/2 cup mayonnaise
- 2 tablespoons Dijon mustard
- 1 tablespoon red vinegar vinegar
- 1/4 cup sweet pickle relish
- 1/4 cup chopped fresh dill
- 1/4 cup chopped green onions
- Salt and freshly ground black pepper to taste

Preparation:

1. **Cook the Pasta:**

   o Cook the elbow macaroni according to the package instructions, then drain and let cool.

2. **Make the Dressing:**

   o In a bowl, combine mayonnaise, Dijon mustard, red vinegar vinegar, and sweet pickle relish. Stir to combine, then season with salt and pepper.

3. **Assemble the Salad:**

   o In a large bowl, combine the cooled macaroni with the dressing, green onions, and fresh dill. Mix until the pasta is well coated.

4. **Serve:**

   o Chill the macaroni salad in the refrigerator for at least 30 minutes before serving.

Tips & Tricks:

- **Flavor Boost:** Add a little more Dijon mustard for an extra tangy kick.

- **Make-Ahead:** This salad actually tastes better after a few hours of chilling, as the flavors meld together. It can be made a day ahead.

- **Add-ins:** For extra crunch, add diced celery, bell peppers, or hard-boiled eggs to the salad.

These reinvented comfort food dishes prove that nostalgia and creativity can coexist in the kitchen. Flay's spin on mac and cheese, meatloaf, and other classics proves that you can take familiar favorites and make them feel brand new again. With bold flavors, fresh ingredients, and simple yet thoughtful techniques, these recipes are sure to elevate your comfort food game to new heights.

Chapter 7: Flavors from the Grill

Introduction: A Lifelong Love Affair with Fire and Smoke

From the first sizzle of meat hitting a hot grill to the smoky fragrance that wafts through the air as food cooks, grilling is a culinary experience unlike any other. For Bobby Flay, grilling has always been at the heart of his cooking philosophy. The act of cooking over an open flame, coaxing deep, smoky flavors from fresh ingredients, is both an art and a passion. It's a process that speaks to primal instincts, a connection to nature, and the timeless allure of cooking food in its simplest, yet most flavorful, form.

Grilling isn't just about the technique; it's about the emotions it stirs—gatherings with friends, sunny afternoons, and the anticipation of that first bite of perfectly grilled food. Whether it's a steak seared to perfection, a rack of ribs glazed with a tangy barbecue sauce, or shrimp infused with bold spices, grilling has the unique ability to elevate any dish. For Bobby Flay, grilling has always been his way of connecting with food, of experimenting with flavors, and of sharing his love for cooking with others.

This chapter is dedicated to the flavors of the grill. We will explore recipes that range from classic to inventive, each showcasing Bobby Flay's knack for pairing fire and smoke with vibrant ingredients. Whether you're grilling in your backyard or over an open flame on a camping trip, these dishes will bring bold, exciting flavors to your outdoor cooking experiences. And just as important, each recipe will offer tips, tricks, and anecdotes that will help you master the grill and bring out the best in every ingredient.

Grilled Steak with Red Chimichurri Sauce

There's nothing quite like a perfectly grilled steak. The deep, smoky flavor from the grill's heat, combined with the rich, juicy interior of the meat, is a thing of beauty. Bobby Flay's grilled steak recipe takes this classic dish and elevates it with a punchy, zesty chimichurri sauce that adds freshness, acidity, and heat.

Ingredients:

- **For the Steak:**
    - 2 bone-in rib-eye steaks (about 1 ½ inches thick)
    - Olive oil
    - Salt and freshly ground black pepper
    - 2 teaspoons smoked paprika
- **For the Chimichurri Sauce:**
    - 1 cup fresh flat-leaf parsley, chopped
    - 2 tablespoons fresh oregano, chopped
    - 1 small red onion, finely chopped
    - 4 cloves garlic, minced
    - 1 tablespoon red vinegar vinegar
    - ½ teaspoon red pepper flakes (or more for heat)
    - 1/3 cup extra virgin olive oil
    - Salt and freshly ground black pepper to taste

Preparation:

1. **Prepare the Steak:**
    - Preheat your grill to high heat. Brush the steaks with olive oil and sprinkle both sides with salt, pepper, and smoked paprika. Let the steaks rest at room temperature for about 15 minutes before grilling to ensure even cooking.

2. **Make the Chimichurri Sauce:**
    - In a bowl, combine the parsley, oregano, onion, garlic, red vinegar vinegar, and red pepper flakes. Slowly drizzle in the olive oil while

stirring to form a loose, slightly chunky sauce. Season with salt and pepper to taste. Set aside to allow the flavors to meld together.

3. **Grill the Steaks:**

   o Place the steaks on the grill and cook for about 4-5 minutes per side for medium-rare, or adjust the time depending on your desired doneness. For best results, use a meat thermometer: 130°F for medium-rare, 140°F for medium, and 150°F for medium-well.

4. **Rest the Steaks:**

   o Once the steaks are cooked to your liking, remove them from the grill and let them rest for at least 5 minutes. This allows the juices to redistribute throughout the meat.

5. **Serve:**

   o Slice the steak against the grain and serve with a generous drizzle of the chimichurri sauce on top. The freshness of the parsley and the heat from the red pepper flakes create the perfect balance for the rich steak.

Tips & Tricks:

- **Choosing the Steak:** Rib-eye is ideal for grilling because of its marbling, which ensures a juicy, flavorful steak. If you prefer leaner cuts, flank or skirt steak will also work well but may require a bit less cooking time.

- **Chimichurri Variations:** You can experiment with different herbs and flavors. Try adding cilantro for a different twist or a squeeze of lemon juice for extra brightness.

- **Grill Marks:** To achieve beautiful grill marks, ensure that the grill is properly preheated and avoid moving the steak too much while cooking.

Cedar-Planked Salmon with Mango-Avocado Salsa

Grilled fish, especially salmon, takes on an incredible flavor when cooked on a cedar plank. The wood imparts a smoky aroma, while the flesh remains moist and tender. Paired with a bright, fresh mango-avocado salsa, this dish is a celebration of both smoky and sweet flavors.

Ingredients:

- **For the Cedar-Planked Salmon:**
    - 4 salmon fillets (about 6 ounces each)
    - 1 cedar plank (soaked in water for at least 1 hour)
    - 2 tablespoons olive oil
    - Salt and freshly ground black pepper
    - 1 teaspoon lemon zest
    - 1 teaspoon smoked paprika
- **For the Mango-Avocado Salsa:**
    - 1 ripe mango, peeled and diced
    - 1 ripe avocado, peeled, pitted, and diced
    - 1 small red onion, finely chopped
    - 1 jalapeño, seeded and minced
    - 2 tablespoons fresh cilantro, chopped
    - 1 tablespoon lime juice
    - Salt and freshly ground black pepper to taste

Preparation:

1. **Prepare the Cedar Plank:**

o Soak the cedar plank in water for at least 1 hour before grilling. This prevents the wood from burning and helps infuse the fish with a smoky flavor.

2. **Prepare the Salmon:**

   o Preheat your grill to medium-high heat. Brush the salmon fillets with olive oil and season with salt, pepper, lemon zest, and smoked paprika.

3. **Grill the Salmon:**

   o Place the soaked cedar plank on the grill and allow it to heat up for 5 minutes, until it starts to release a fragrant smoky aroma. Place the salmon fillets on the plank, skin-side down. Close the lid of the grill and cook for about 12-15 minutes, or until the salmon is cooked through and flakes easily with a fork.

4. **Make the Salsa:**

   o While the salmon is grilling, combine the mango, avocado, red onion, jalapeño, cilantro, and lime juice in a bowl. Season with salt and pepper to taste. Set aside.

5. **Serve:**

   o Once the salmon is ready, remove it from the grill and serve with a generous scoop of the mango-avocado salsa on top. The sweetness of the mango and the creaminess of the avocado perfectly complement the smoky salmon.

Tips & Tricks:

- **Cedar Plank Alternatives:** If you can't find a cedar plank, you can use other types of wood like alder or hickory. Just ensure that the wood is safe for grilling.

- **Grill Lid:** Always keep the lid closed while cooking the salmon on the cedar plank to help it cook evenly and maintain moisture.

- **Salsa Variations:** You can add other fruits to the salsa, such as pineapple or papaya, for a tropical twist.

Grilled Lamb with Rosemary-Lemon Marinade

Grilled lamb, with its rich and slightly gamey flavor, is a favorite in many cultures, and Bobby Flay's rosemary-lemon marinade brings out its best. The marinade infuses the lamb with fresh, aromatic herbs, bright lemon, and a touch of garlic, creating a deliciously flavorful dish.

Ingredients:

- 4 lamb chops (about 1 inch thick)
- 3 tablespoons olive oil
- 1 tablespoon fresh rosemary, chopped
- Zest and juice of 1 lemon
- 2 garlic cloves, minced
- Salt and freshly ground black pepper

Preparation:

1. **Marinate the Lamb:**
   - In a small bowl, combine the olive oil, rosemary, lemon zest, lemon juice, garlic, salt, and pepper. Place the lamb chops in a shallow dish and pour the marinade over them. Cover and refrigerate for at least 30 minutes, or up to 2 hours.

2. **Grill the Lamb:**
   - Preheat your grill to medium-high heat. Remove the lamb chops from the marinade and season them with additional salt and pepper. Grill the lamb for about 4-5 minutes per side for medium-rare, or adjust the time for your preferred doneness.

3. **Rest the Lamb:**

   o Let the lamb chops rest for 5 minutes before serving to allow the juices to redistribute.

4. **Serve:**

   o Serve the lamb chops with a drizzle of olive oil and a sprinkle of fresh rosemary.

Tips & Tricks:

- **Doneness:** Use a meat thermometer to check for doneness: 130°F for medium-rare, 140°F for medium, and 150°F for medium-well.

- **Marinade Time:** Don't marinate the lamb too long, as the acid from the lemon can begin to break down the meat, making it mushy.

Spicy Grilled Shrimp with Cilantro Pesto

Shrimp grills quickly, and when paired with a fiery, flavorful cilantro pesto, it becomes a perfect bite of smoky, herby, and spicy goodness. Bobby Flay's spicy grilled shrimp recipe is an excellent example of how simple ingredients can create bold, complex flavors.

Ingredients:

- 1 pound large shrimp, peeled and deveined

- 2 tablespoons olive oil

- 1 teaspoon smoked paprika

- 1 teaspoon chili powder

- Salt and freshly ground black pepper

- **For the Cilantro Pesto:**

  o 1 bunch fresh cilantro, chopped

- 1/4 cup pine nuts
- 2 garlic cloves, minced
- 1/2 cup extra virgin olive oil
- Juice of 1 lime
- Salt to taste

Preparation:

1. **Prepare the Shrimp:**
   - In a bowl, combine the shrimp with olive oil, smoked paprika, chili powder, salt, and pepper. Toss to coat the shrimp evenly.

2. **Make the Cilantro Pesto:**
   - In a food processor, combine the cilantro, pine nuts, garlic, and olive oil. Process until smooth, then add the lime juice and salt to taste.

3. **Grill the Shrimp:**
   - Preheat your grill to medium-high heat. Thread the shrimp onto skewers and grill for about 2-3 minutes per side, or until they are opaque and slightly charred.

4. **Serve:**
   - Serve the grilled shrimp with a generous drizzle of cilantro pesto.

Tips & Tricks:

- **Shrimp Skewers:** Soak wooden skewers in water for 30 minutes before using to prevent them from burning on the grill.
- **Adjusting Heat:** If you like it spicier, add more chili powder or a chopped fresh jalapeño to the pesto.

Barbecue Ribs with Pineapple-Mango Glaze

When it comes to grilling, few things are as satisfying as a rack of tender, smoky ribs. Bobby Flay's barbecue ribs are glazed with a tropical pineapple-mango sauce that adds sweetness and a bit of spice to every bite.

Ingredients:

- 1 rack of baby back ribs
- Salt and freshly ground black pepper
- 1 tablespoon olive oil
- **For the Pineapple-Mango Glaze:**
    - 1 cup pineapple juice
    - 1/2 cup mango puree
    - 2 tablespoons brown sugar
    - 1 tablespoon apple cider vinegar
    - 1 teaspoon chili flakes

Preparation:

1. **Prepare the Ribs:**
    - Preheat your grill to medium-low heat. Rub the ribs with salt, pepper, and olive oil.

2. **Make the Glaze:**
    - In a saucepan, combine the pineapple juice, mango puree, brown sugar, apple cider vinegar, and chili flakes. Simmer over low heat for 10-15 minutes, until thickened.

3. **Grill the Ribs:**
    - Place the ribs on the grill and cook for 2-3 hours over indirect heat, basting with the glaze every 30 minutes. The ribs are done

when they are tender and the meat easily pulls away from the bone.

4. **Serve:**

   o   Slice the ribs and serve with additional glaze on the side.

Tips & Tricks:

- **Indirect Heat:** For tender ribs, use indirect heat on the grill, which ensures slow cooking and allows the ribs to become tender without burning.

- **Glaze Adjustments:** If you want more heat, add a little bit of chopped jalapeño or hot sauce to the glaze for an extra kick.

This chapter has covered a wide array of flavors from the grill, from steak and seafood to lamb and ribs. Grilling is a technique that brings out the best in ingredients, infusing them with a smoky flavor that is unmatched by any other cooking method. Each recipe offers its own unique experience and presents opportunities for you to experiment and make each dish your own. Whether you're grilling for a family dinner or hosting a summer barbecue, these recipes will ensure your grill is the centerpiece of every delicious meal.

Chapter 8: Global Inspirations

Introduction: A World of Flavors on a Plate

The beauty of cooking lies not only in the ingredients you use but also in the stories and cultures that they carry. Throughout his career, Bobby Flay has constantly sought inspiration from around the world, blending traditional techniques with his bold, modern approach. This chapter takes us on a culinary journey, showcasing dishes influenced by diverse global flavors—from the fiery heat of Korean barbecue to the aromatic spices of Morocco and India.

Bobby Flay's philosophy is simple: great food is about using the best ingredients and preparing them in a way that allows their inherent flavors to shine. Whether grilling, searing, or simmering, each of these recipes has been carefully crafted to bring the best of international flavors into your kitchen. Each dish tells a story, and it's through cooking that we can explore different cultures, their culinary techniques, and the heart of their food.

In this chapter, you will learn how to prepare dishes that offer a beautiful fusion of bold spices, fresh ingredients, and vibrant sauces. The goal is to bring the world to your plate, creating meals that transport you to distant lands with every bite.

Grilled Korean-Style Short Ribs with Kimchi

Korean barbecue is a global sensation, known for its vibrant, umami-rich flavors and the smoky aroma that fills the air when the meat hits the grill. Flay's take on Korean-style short ribs is infused with traditional ingredients like soy sauce, sesame oil, garlic, and brown sugar, making this dish a perfect introduction to the world of Korean grilling.

Ingredients:

- **For the Short Ribs:**

- 3 pounds of beef short ribs, cut into thin strips across the bone
- 1/4 cup soy sauce
- 2 tablespoons sesame oil
- 2 tablespoons rice vinegar
- 1 tablespoon brown sugar
- 3 cloves garlic, minced
- 2 tablespoons grated fresh ginger
- 2 tablespoons green onions, finely chopped
- 1 tablespoon toasted sesame seeds
- 1/2 teaspoon black pepper

- **For the Kimchi:**
    - 1 medium napa cabbage, chopped
    - 2 tablespoons sea salt
    - 1 tablespoon grated ginger
    - 2 cloves garlic, minced
    - 1 tablespoon gochugaru (Korean chili flakes)
    - 2 tablespoons fish sauce
    - 1 tablespoon rice vinegar
    - 1 tablespoon sugar
    - 1/2 cup chopped green onions

Preparation:

1. **Marinate the Short Ribs:**
    - In a bowl, combine the soy sauce, sesame oil, rice vinegar, brown sugar, garlic, ginger, green onions, sesame seeds, and black pepper. Whisk together until the sugar dissolves. Place the short

ribs in a large resealable plastic bag or shallow dish and pour the marinade over them. Seal the bag and refrigerate for at least 2 hours, or overnight for the best flavor.

2. **Make the Kimchi:**

   - Begin by sprinkling the napa cabbage with sea salt and letting it sit for 1-2 hours, allowing it to wilt. After the cabbage softens, rinse it thoroughly to remove excess salt. In a mixing bowl, combine ginger, garlic, gochugaru, fish sauce, rice vinegar, and sugar. Add the cabbage and green onions to the mixture and toss everything together, making sure the cabbage is evenly coated. Let the kimchi sit for 24 hours at room temperature to ferment before refrigerating.

3. **Grill the Short Ribs:**

   - Preheat your grill to medium-high heat. Place the marinated short ribs on the grill and cook for 3-4 minutes per side, or until they are caramelized and slightly charred. Be sure to brush the ribs with any remaining marinade during grilling for extra flavor.

4. **Serve:**

   - Remove the short ribs from the grill and let them rest for a few minutes. Serve them with a generous helping of homemade kimchi on the side for a perfect pairing of smoky, savory, and spicy flavors.

Tips & Tricks:

- **Marinating Time:** The longer the short ribs marinate, the more flavorful they become. If you have the time, marinate them overnight.

- **Kimchi Fermentation:** The kimchi's flavors deepen the longer it ferments. Start it a day ahead for the best results.

- **Grill Temperature:** Don't overcrowd the grill. Allow the short ribs space to cook evenly and achieve that perfect char.

Thai Beef Salad with Lime and Thai Basil

The Thai beef salad is a refreshing, zesty dish that balances the deep flavors of seared beef with the bright, vibrant notes of lime, mint, and Thai basil. It's a perfect example of how fresh herbs and tangy dressings can elevate a simple salad into a memorable meal.

Ingredients:

- **For the Salad:**
  - 1 lb flank steak, grilled and thinly sliced
  - 4 cups mixed greens (such as arugula or spinach)
  - 1 cucumber, thinly sliced
  - 1 red bell pepper, thinly sliced
  - 1/2 red onion, thinly sliced
  - 1/2 cup fresh cilantro leaves
  - 1/4 cup fresh Thai basil leaves
  - 1/4 cup fresh mint leaves
  - 2 tablespoons chopped roasted peanuts (for garnish)
- **For the Dressing:**
  - 2 tablespoons fish sauce
  - 2 tablespoons lime juice
  - 1 tablespoon sugar
  - 1 small red chili, minced
  - 1 tablespoon rice vinegar
  - 1 tablespoon sesame oil
  - 1 garlic clove, minced

Preparation:

1. **Grill the Beef:**

   o Preheat your grill to medium-high heat. Season the flank steak with salt and pepper and grill it for about 4-5 minutes per side for medium-rare. Once cooked, remove from the grill and let it rest for 5 minutes before slicing it thinly against the grain.

2. **Make the Dressing:**

   o In a small bowl, whisk together the fish sauce, lime juice, sugar, minced chili, rice vinegar, sesame oil, and garlic. Stir until the sugar dissolves completely.

3. **Assemble the Salad:**

   o In a large bowl, toss together the mixed greens, cucumber, bell pepper, red onion, cilantro, Thai basil, and mint. Add the sliced beef on top and pour the dressing over everything. Toss gently to combine.

4. **Serve:**

   o Serve the salad in individual bowls, garnishing with chopped peanuts for crunch. The result is a refreshing salad that balances spicy, tangy, and savory notes in every bite.

Tips & Tricks:

- **Meat Alternatives:** If you prefer another cut of beef, sirloin or rib-eye will also work well. Just be sure to grill it to your preferred level of doneness.

- **Herb Substitutes:** If you can't find Thai basil, regular basil can work in a pinch, but Thai basil has a distinct flavor that's key to the authenticity of the dish.

- **Spice Level:** Adjust the amount of chili in the dressing according to your heat preference.

Grilled Tuna with Soy-Ginger Marinade and Pickled Cucumbers

Grilled tuna is a perfect balance of smoky and tender, and when paired with a soy-ginger marinade, it becomes an unforgettable dish. Add the tang of pickled cucumbers, and you've got a meal that marries rich, savory flavors with refreshing acidity.

Ingredients:

- **For the Tuna:**
    - 4 tuna steaks (about 6 ounces each)
    - 2 tablespoons soy sauce
    - 2 tablespoons sesame oil
    - 2 tablespoons rice vinegar
    - 1 tablespoon grated ginger
    - 1 tablespoon honey
    - 1 tablespoon green onions, chopped
    - 1 clove garlic, minced
- **For the Pickled Cucumbers:**
    - 1 cucumber, thinly sliced
    - 1/2 cup rice vinegar
    - 1 tablespoon sugar
    - 1/2 teaspoon salt
    - 1/4 teaspoon red pepper flakes

Preparation:

1. **Make the Marinade:**

- In a bowl, combine the soy sauce, sesame oil, rice vinegar, ginger, honey, green onions, and garlic. Whisk together to combine.

2. **Marinate the Tuna:**

   - Place the tuna steaks in a shallow dish and pour the marinade over them. Let the tuna marinate in the refrigerator for 30 minutes to 1 hour.

3. **Pickle the Cucumbers:**

   - In a separate bowl, combine the rice vinegar, sugar, salt, and red pepper flakes. Stir until the sugar and salt dissolve. Add the cucumber slices and allow them to sit in the brine for 30 minutes.

4. **Grill the Tuna:**

   - Preheat your grill to high heat. Remove the tuna steaks from the marinade and place them on the grill. Grill for 2-3 minutes per side for medium-rare, or longer if you prefer your tuna more cooked.

5. **Serve:**

   - Serve the grilled tuna with a side of pickled cucumbers for a burst of freshness and acidity.

Tips & Tricks:

- **Tuna Preparation:** Make sure not to overcook the tuna, as it can dry out. The goal is to achieve a crispy exterior while keeping the center tender and rare.

- **Pickled Cucumbers:** If you prefer a milder pickle, reduce the amount of red pepper flakes or omit them entirely.

Moroccan Spiced Chicken with Couscous

Moroccan cuisine is rich in spices, and this dish brings together the warmth of cumin, coriander, and cinnamon to flavor chicken, served with a fragrant couscous that absorbs all of the delicious spices.

Ingredients:

- **For the Chicken:**
    - 4 bone-in, skin-on chicken thighs
    - 2 teaspoons ground cumin
    - 1 teaspoon ground coriander
    - 1 teaspoon ground cinnamon
    - 1 teaspoon paprika
    - Salt and freshly ground black pepper
    - 2 tablespoons olive oil

- **For the Couscous:**
    - 1 cup couscous
    - 1 tablespoon olive oil
    - 1 cup chicken broth
    - 1/2 teaspoon ground cumin
    - 1/2 teaspoon ground coriander
    - 1/4 cup dried apricots, chopped
    - 1/4 cup toasted almonds, chopped
    - Fresh cilantro for garnish

Preparation:

1. **Season the Chicken:**

- o In a small bowl, combine the cumin, coriander, cinnamon, paprika, salt, and pepper. Rub the chicken thighs with olive oil and then sprinkle the spice mixture over them, ensuring they are evenly coated.

2. **Cook the Chicken:**

   - o Heat a large skillet over medium-high heat. Add the chicken thighs and cook for 6-7 minutes per side, until the skin is crispy and the chicken is cooked through.

3. **Prepare the Couscous:**

   - o In a separate saucepan, bring the chicken broth to a boil. Stir in the couscous, olive oil, cumin, and coriander. Cover the pan and remove from heat, allowing the couscous to steam for about 5 minutes. Fluff with a fork and stir in the apricots and almonds.

4. **Serve:**

   - o Serve the chicken thighs over the couscous, garnished with fresh cilantro.

Tips & Tricks:

- • **Chicken Cooking:** Bone-in, skin-on chicken thighs are ideal for this recipe because they stay moist and flavorful during cooking.

- • **Couscous Variations:** For a variation, you can use quinoa or farro in place of couscous for a heartier base.

Indian-Style Shrimp Curry with Cardamom Rice

Indian cuisine offers a bounty of aromatic spices, and this shrimp curry highlights the warmth of cardamom and the richness of coconut milk. Paired with cardamom rice, this dish brings the deep flavors of India right to your table.

Ingredients:

- **For the Shrimp Curry:**
    - 1 lb large shrimp, peeled and deveined
    - 1 tablespoon ghee (or vegetable oil)
    - 1 medium onion, finely chopped
    - 2 garlic cloves, minced
    - 1-inch piece of ginger, grated
    - 2 teaspoons ground cumin
    - 1 teaspoon ground turmeric
    - 1 teaspoon ground coriander
    - 1 teaspoon garam masala
    - 1 can (14 oz) coconut milk
    - 1/2 cup diced tomatoes
    - Fresh cilantro for garnish
    - Salt to taste
- **For the Cardamom Rice:**
    - 1 cup basmati rice
    - 1/2 teaspoon ground cardamom
    - 2 cups water
    - 1 tablespoon ghee or butter
    - Salt to taste

Preparation:

1. **Make the Rice:**

- Rinse the basmati rice under cold water until the water runs clear. In a saucepan, heat the ghee or butter over medium heat. Add the cardamom and toast it for a minute before adding the rice. Stir for a minute to coat the rice in the spices, then add the water and salt. Bring to a boil, reduce the heat to low, and cover the saucepan. Cook for 15-20 minutes, until the rice is tender.

2. **Prepare the Shrimp Curry:**

   - Heat the ghee or oil in a large skillet over medium heat. Add the onion, garlic, and ginger, cooking for 5-7 minutes until softened. Add the cumin, turmeric, coriander, and garam masala, and cook for another minute until fragrant. Add the coconut milk and tomatoes, bringing it to a simmer. Add the shrimp and cook for 4-5 minutes, until they are pink and cooked through.

3. **Serve:**

   - Serve the shrimp curry over the cardamom rice and garnish with fresh cilantro.

Tips & Tricks:

- **Shrimp Cooking:** Be careful not to overcook the shrimp, as they can become rubbery. Once they turn pink and opaque, they are done.

- **Spice Adjustments:** If you prefer a milder curry, reduce the amount of garam masala or cumin.

This chapter brings the world to your kitchen, blending international flavors with Bobby Flay's bold, modern techniques. Each dish allows you to explore new culinary landscapes while enjoying the familiar joy of cooking with family and friends.

Chapter 9: Sweets and Indulgences

Introduction: Flay's Sweet Finale

After a meal filled with bold flavors and complex combinations, dessert is the moment where we indulge, relax, and savor the final tastes of the evening. For Bobby Flay, desserts are an opportunity to showcase creativity, balance, and, most importantly, flavor. His approach to sweets often involves a playful balance of unexpected flavors, textures, and familiar classics given a modern twist. In this chapter, we explore some of his most beloved and indulgent dessert recipes, which showcase his culinary creativity and passion for elevating simple ingredients into unforgettable finales.

Desserts are more than just a sweet treat; they are a celebration of the meal that came before them. Whether it's a decadent chocolate cake with a kick of chili, a tangy key lime pie with a toasted coconut crust, or a delicate panna cotta with a fresh blueberry compote, Bobby Flay's desserts are designed to create lasting memories. His combination of spices, textures, and technique pushes the boundaries of what a dessert can be.

Let's dive into these five exceptional desserts that offer a range of flavors—from the deep richness of chocolate to the zesty brightness of citrus. Each recipe is a journey into the world of sweets, with step-by-step instructions, tips, and tricks to ensure you can recreate these indulgences at home.

Chocolate Cake with Cinnamon-Chili Whipped Cream

When it comes to indulgence, nothing beats a rich, decadent chocolate cake. But Bobby Flay's version takes this classic dessert to the next level by pairing it with a spicy-sweet cinnamon-chili whipped cream that adds an unexpected kick to every bite. This cake combines the richness of chocolate with the complexity of spices for a dessert that is as exciting as it is comforting.

Ingredients:

- **For the Cake:**
  - 1 3/4 cups all-purpose flour
  - 1 1/2 teaspoons baking powder
  - 1/2 teaspoon baking soda
  - 1/4 teaspoon salt
  - 1/2 cup unsweetened cocoa powder
  - 3/4 cup granulated sugar
  - 3/4 cup packed brown sugar
  - 3/4 cup vegetable oil
  - 2 large eggs
  - 1 teaspoon vanilla extract
  - 1 cup buttermilk
  - 1/2 cup hot water
- **For the Cinnamon-Chili Whipped Cream:**
  - 1 cup heavy cream
  - 1 tablespoon powdered sugar
  - 1 teaspoon ground cinnamon
  - 1/2 teaspoon chili powder (or more, depending on your spice tolerance)
  - 1/4 teaspoon vanilla extract

Preparation:

1. **Make the Cake:**
   - Preheat your oven to 350°F (175°C). Grease and flour two 9-inch round cake pans.

- In a medium bowl, whisk together the flour, baking powder, baking soda, salt, and cocoa powder.

- In a large bowl, whisk together the granulated sugar, brown sugar, oil, eggs, and vanilla extract until smooth. Add the dry ingredients to the wet ingredients in batches, alternating with the buttermilk. Be sure to start and end with the dry ingredients. Mix until just combined.

- Add the hot water to the batter and mix until smooth. The batter will be quite thin, but that's perfectly fine.

- Divide the batter evenly between the prepared cake pans and bake for 30-35 minutes, or until a toothpick inserted into the center comes out clean. Let the cakes cool in the pans for 10 minutes before transferring them to wire racks to cool completely.

2. **Make the Whipped Cream:**

- In a medium bowl, whisk together the heavy cream, powdered sugar, cinnamon, chili powder, and vanilla extract. Whisk until soft peaks form. Taste and adjust the level of spice by adding more chili powder if desired.

3. **Assemble the Cake:**

- Once the cakes are completely cool, place one layer on a serving platter. Spread a generous amount of whipped cream on top of the first layer. Place the second cake on top and finish with more whipped cream.

- If desired, garnish the cake with a sprinkle of cinnamon or a few dried chili flakes for an added touch of drama.

Tips & Tricks:

- **Spice Level:** Adjust the level of chili powder based on your spice tolerance. Start with a small amount and gradually add more to find your ideal balance.

- **Moisture:** The addition of hot water in the batter ensures a moist cake, so don't skip this step.
- **Whipped Cream:** Make sure the heavy cream is very cold before whipping for the best results.

Banana Pudding with Salted Caramel

Banana pudding is a nostalgic Southern dessert, but Bobby Flay adds a luxurious twist by pairing it with salted caramel, creating a perfect balance of sweet and salty flavors. The rich custard, layered with creamy whipped cream, bananas, and a drizzle of homemade salted caramel, creates a decadent dessert that's impossible to resist.

Ingredients:

- **For the Custard:**
  - 4 large egg yolks
  - 1/2 cup granulated sugar
  - 2 tablespoons cornstarch
  - 2 cups whole milk
  - 1 teaspoon vanilla extract

- **For the Salted Caramel:**
  - 1/2 cup granulated sugar
  - 2 tablespoons unsalted butter
  - 1/4 cup heavy cream
  - 1/2 teaspoon sea salt

- **For the Assembly:**
  - 4 ripe bananas, sliced
  - 1 box of vanilla wafers

- o 1 cup heavy cream
- o 2 tablespoons powdered sugar

Preparation:

1. **Make the Custard:**
   - o In a medium saucepan, whisk together the egg yolks, sugar, and cornstarch until smooth. Gradually whisk in the milk, then place the saucepan over medium heat. Cook, whisking constantly, until the mixture thickens and comes to a simmer. This should take about 5-7 minutes.
   - o Once thickened, remove from heat and stir in the vanilla extract. Let the custard cool slightly, then cover with plastic wrap and refrigerate until fully chilled, about 2 hours.

2. **Make the Salted Caramel:**
   - o In a small saucepan, melt the sugar over medium heat until it turns a golden amber color. Be sure to stir constantly to prevent burning.
   - o Once the sugar has melted, add the butter and stir until smooth. Gradually add the heavy cream, stirring constantly. Be careful, as the mixture will bubble up. Stir in the sea salt and remove from heat. Let the caramel cool to room temperature.

3. **Assemble the Banana Pudding:**
   - o In a large bowl, whip the heavy cream and powdered sugar until soft peaks form. In a separate bowl, fold the whipped cream into the chilled custard.
   - o In individual serving glasses or a large trifle dish, layer the vanilla wafers, sliced bananas, and custard mixture. Repeat the layers, finishing with a layer of custard on top.
   - o Drizzle with salted caramel and refrigerate for at least 2 hours before serving to allow the flavors to meld together.

Tips & Tricks:

- **Custard Texture:** Be sure to whisk constantly while cooking the custard to avoid curdling the eggs.

- **Caramel Storage:** You can store leftover salted caramel in the refrigerator for up to a week. Reheat gently before using.

- **Bananas:** For best results, slice the bananas just before assembling to avoid them turning brown.

Lemon-Buttermilk Panna Cotta with Blueberry Compote

Panna cotta is a classic Italian dessert that's simple yet elegant. Bobby Flay's version uses buttermilk for a tangy twist, while the lemon adds a bright freshness. Topped with a blueberry compote, this panna cotta is light, creamy, and full of flavor.

Ingredients:

- **For the Panna Cotta:**
  - 2 cups heavy cream
  - 1/2 cup buttermilk
  - 1/4 cup granulated sugar
  - Zest of 1 lemon
  - 1 teaspoon vanilla extract
  - 2 teaspoons gelatin
  - 2 tablespoons cold water
- **For the Blueberry Compote:**
  - 2 cups fresh blueberries
  - 1/4 cup granulated sugar

- o 1 tablespoon lemon juice
- o 1 teaspoon lemon zest

Preparation:

1. **Make the Panna Cotta:**

   - o In a small bowl, sprinkle the gelatin over the cold water and let it bloom for 5 minutes.

   - o In a saucepan, heat the heavy cream, buttermilk, sugar, lemon zest, and vanilla extract over medium heat. Stir occasionally until the sugar dissolves and the mixture is hot but not boiling.

   - o Remove from heat and stir in the gelatin until fully dissolved. Pour the mixture into serving glasses or ramekins and refrigerate for at least 4 hours, or overnight, until set.

2. **Make the Blueberry Compote:**

   - o In a small saucepan, combine the blueberries, sugar, lemon juice, and lemon zest. Cook over medium heat, stirring occasionally, until the berries begin to release their juices and the mixture thickens, about 10 minutes.

   - o Let the compote cool to room temperature.

3. **Serve:**

   - o Once the panna cotta has set, spoon a generous amount of the blueberry compote over the top and serve.

Tips & Tricks:

- • **Gelatin Blooming:** Be sure to let the gelatin bloom in cold water before adding it to the hot cream mixture to ensure it dissolves properly.

- • **Compote Variations:** Feel free to swap the blueberries for other berries, such as raspberries or blackberries.

These are just a few of Bobby Flay's indulgent desserts that bring a creative twist to classic sweets. Each recipe emphasizes balance and flavor, inviting you to explore new techniques and flavors. Whether you're making a spicy chocolate cake or a tangy panna cotta, these desserts will leave you and your guests craving more.

Chapter 10: Entertaining and Holiday Feasts

Introduction: Creating Memorable Meals for Friends and Family

Cooking for friends and family is a deeply personal and rewarding experience. It's about more than just preparing a meal; it's about creating memories and moments that bring people together. When Bobby Flay steps into the kitchen to prepare a meal for those he loves, his goal is always to elevate the experience through bold, thoughtful flavors, innovative techniques, and dishes that make everyone at the table feel special.

Entertaining is about more than just the food itself—it's about setting the scene, creating an atmosphere where guests feel welcome, and making sure the meal flows with ease. For Flay, these dishes aren't just food—they're a representation of joy, shared moments, and the beauty of hospitality. Whether you're hosting a formal holiday dinner, a casual gathering, or a special occasion, the goal is always the same: to create a feast that feels extraordinary while still being approachable and enjoyable for everyone.

This chapter focuses on some of Bobby Flay's most beloved recipes for entertaining and holiday feasts. These dishes reflect the essence of great cooking—rich flavors, beautiful presentations, and a balance of tradition and innovation. From a perfectly roasted beef tenderloin to a show-stopping roasted rack of lamb, these recipes are designed to impress and create lasting memories.

We will dive deep into each of these dishes, exploring their origins, techniques, and the tricks Bobby Flay uses to make them stand out. Along the way, we'll share helpful tips, tricks, and personal anecdotes that will help you recreate these dishes with confidence in your own kitchen.

Roasted Beef Tenderloin with Horseradish Cream

A perfect beef tenderloin is one of the most luxurious dishes you can serve at any holiday feast or celebration. With its rich, buttery texture and succulent flavor, beef tenderloin is a showstopper, especially when paired with a zesty horseradish cream. Bobby Flay's version of this dish is simple, yet sophisticated, allowing the natural flavors of the beef to shine while adding the sharp contrast of horseradish to cut through the richness.

Ingredients:

- **For the Beef Tenderloin:**
  - 1 whole beef tenderloin (about 4-5 pounds), trimmed of silver skin
  - 2 tablespoons olive oil
  - 3 cloves garlic, minced
  - 2 tablespoons fresh rosemary, finely chopped
  - 1 tablespoon fresh thyme leaves, chopped
  - 1 teaspoon kosher salt
  - 1/2 teaspoon freshly ground black pepper
- **For the Horseradish Cream:**
  - 1/2 cup sour cream
  - 1/4 cup prepared horseradish (adjust to your taste)
  - 1 tablespoon Dijon mustard
  - 1 tablespoon fresh lemon juice
  - Salt and pepper to taste

Preparation:

1. **Prepare the Beef:**

- o Preheat your oven to 425°F (220°C). Place the tenderloin on a clean surface and rub it with the olive oil, garlic, rosemary, thyme, salt, and pepper. Be sure to coat the meat evenly for maximum flavor.

- o Heat a large oven-safe skillet over medium-high heat. When hot, add the beef tenderloin and sear it on all sides for 3-4 minutes, until the exterior is browned and caramelized.

2. **Roast the Beef:**

- o Transfer the skillet to the preheated oven and roast the beef for 20-25 minutes for medium-rare, or longer for your desired doneness. The key here is to monitor the internal temperature with a meat thermometer—125°F for medium-rare, 135°F for medium.

- o Once the beef has reached your desired temperature, remove it from the oven and let it rest for at least 10-15 minutes before slicing. Resting allows the juices to redistribute, ensuring a juicy and tender roast.

3. **Make the Horseradish Cream:**

- o In a small bowl, mix together the sour cream, horseradish, Dijon mustard, lemon juice, salt, and pepper. Adjust the horseradish to your liking for more or less heat.

- o Serve the beef sliced with a generous dollop of horseradish cream on the side.

Tips & Tricks:

- **Perfect Sear:** Searing the beef tenderloin before roasting ensures a rich, flavorful crust. Don't skip this step, as it enhances the flavor profile of the roast.

- **Horseradish Adjustments:** If you prefer a milder sauce, use a little less horseradish, or even mix in some cream cheese or mascarpone for a softer flavor.

- **Resting the Meat:** Always rest the beef after roasting to allow the juices to redistribute, keeping the meat tender and juicy.

Crab Cakes with Lemon-Dill Aioli

Crab cakes are a crowd favorite for their delicate seafood flavor, crunchy exterior, and rich, savory filling. Bobby Flay's crab cakes are packed with lump crab meat and seasoned with fresh herbs, then served with a tangy lemon-dill aioli that adds an extra layer of brightness. These crab cakes are perfect as appetizers or as part of a larger holiday spread.

Ingredients:

- **For the Crab Cakes:**
  - 1 pound lump crab meat (fresh or canned, drained and picked over)
  - 1/2 cup fresh breadcrumbs
  - 2 tablespoons mayonnaise
  - 1 egg
  - 2 teaspoons Dijon mustard
  - 1 tablespoon fresh parsley, finely chopped
  - 1 tablespoon fresh chives, finely chopped
  - 1 teaspoon Old Bay seasoning
  - 1/2 teaspoon lemon zest
  - Salt and pepper to taste
  - 2 tablespoons vegetable oil, for frying
- **For the Lemon-Dill Aioli:**
  - 1/2 cup mayonnaise
  - 2 tablespoons fresh lemon juice

- o 1 tablespoon Dijon mustard
- o 2 teaspoons fresh dill, chopped
- o Salt and pepper to taste

Preparation:

1. **Make the Crab Cake Mixture:**
   - o In a large bowl, gently mix together the crab meat, breadcrumbs, mayonnaise, egg, Dijon mustard, parsley, chives, Old Bay seasoning, lemon zest, salt, and pepper. Be careful not to break up the crab meat too much—large lumps will give the crab cakes a better texture.
   - o Form the mixture into small patties, about 3 inches in diameter, and set them aside.

2. **Make the Aioli:**
   - o In a small bowl, whisk together the mayonnaise, lemon juice, Dijon mustard, dill, salt, and pepper. Taste and adjust the seasoning, adding more lemon juice or mustard for tang if needed.

3. **Cook the Crab Cakes:**
   - o Heat the vegetable oil in a large skillet over medium heat. Once the oil is hot, add the crab cakes in batches, being careful not to overcrowd the pan.
   - o Cook for about 3-4 minutes per side, until golden brown and crisp. Once cooked, transfer the crab cakes to a paper towel-lined plate to drain excess oil.

4. **Serve:**
   - o Serve the crab cakes hot with a generous dollop of lemon-dill aioli on the side.

Tips & Tricks:

- **Fresh Crab Meat:** If you can find fresh lump crab meat, it will elevate these crab cakes significantly. Canned crab meat can work in a pinch, but fresh crab provides the best flavor and texture.

- **Frying Tips:** Make sure the oil is hot before adding the crab cakes to avoid sticking. If the oil is too cold, the cakes will absorb excess oil and become greasy.

- **Aioli Variations:** You can add a bit of garlic to the aioli for a deeper flavor, or substitute the dill with tarragon or parsley for a different herbal note.

Grilled Vegetable Platter with Garlic Herb Vinaigrette

A beautiful vegetable platter is a fantastic way to offer a lighter, fresh counterpoint to rich meats in a holiday spread. Bobby Flay's grilled vegetable platter is a mix of seasonal vegetables like bell peppers, zucchini, and eggplant, simply grilled and topped with a garlic herb vinaigrette. This dish is light, flavorful, and perfect for entertaining guests who prefer plant-based options.

Ingredients:

- **For the Vegetables:**
  - 2 zucchini, sliced into 1/4-inch thick rounds
  - 2 yellow squash, sliced into 1/4-inch thick rounds
  - 2 bell peppers (red or yellow), cut into large chunks
  - 1 eggplant, sliced into 1/4-inch thick rounds
  - 1 red onion, sliced into thick rounds
  - Olive oil for drizzling
  - Salt and freshly ground black pepper

- **For the Garlic Herb Vinaigrette:**

- 1/4 cup red vinegar vinegar
- 1 tablespoon Dijon mustard
- 2 cloves garlic, minced
- 1/4 cup fresh parsley, chopped
- 1/4 cup fresh basil, chopped
- 1/4 cup extra virgin olive oil
- Salt and pepper to taste

Preparation:

1. **Prepare the Vegetables:**
   - Preheat your grill or grill pan to medium-high heat. Drizzle the zucchini, squash, bell peppers, eggplant, and onion with olive oil, then season with salt and pepper.
   - Grill the vegetables in batches, cooking each side for 3-4 minutes until they are tender and have grill marks. Be sure not to overcrowd the grill so each piece cooks evenly.

2. **Make the Vinaigrette:**
   - In a small bowl, whisk together the red vinegar vinegar, Dijon mustard, garlic, parsley, basil, and olive oil. Season with salt and pepper to taste.

3. **Assemble and Serve:**
   - Arrange the grilled vegetables on a large platter. Drizzle the garlic herb vinaigrette over the top, and serve warm or at room temperature.

Tips & Tricks:

- **Vegetable Choices:** Feel free to swap in other vegetables based on availability and personal preferences, such as mushrooms, asparagus, or carrots.

- **Grill Marks:** To get beautiful grill marks, make sure the grill is hot enough, and try not to move the vegetables around too much while cooking.

- **Vinaigrette Variations:** For a deeper flavor, try adding a bit of balsamic vinegar to the vinaigrette or substituting lemon juice for the red vinegar vinegar for a fresher, brighter taste.

Thanksgiving Turkey with Cider Gravy

No holiday meal is complete without a beautifully roasted turkey, and Bobby Flay's version incorporates apple cider into both the turkey and the gravy, lending a touch of sweetness and acidity that perfectly complements the rich, savory bird.

Ingredients:

- **For the Turkey:**
  - 1 whole turkey (12-14 pounds)
  - 2 tablespoons olive oil
  - 2 teaspoons kosher salt
  - 1 teaspoon freshly ground black pepper
  - 1 lemon, halved
  - 2 sprigs rosemary
  - 1 onion, quartered
  - 4 cloves garlic, smashed
  - 2 cups apple cider (for basting)

- **For the Cider Gravy:**

- 1/4 cup unsalted butter
- 1/4 cup all-purpose flour
- 2 cups turkey stock
- 1/2 cup apple cider
- Salt and pepper to taste

Preparation:

1. **Prepare the Turkey:**
   - Preheat the oven to 325°F (165°C). Pat the turkey dry with paper towels and season it inside and out with salt and pepper. Stuff the cavity with lemon halves, rosemary sprigs, onion, and garlic.
   - Rub the turkey with olive oil and place it on a rack in a roasting pan. Pour 1 cup of apple cider into the bottom of the pan.

2. **Roast the Turkey:**
   - Roast the turkey for 2 1/2 to 3 hours, basting it every 30 minutes with the remaining apple cider. Use a meat thermometer to check for doneness—when the internal temperature reaches 165°F (74°C) in the thickest part of the thigh, the turkey is done.

3. **Make the Gravy:**
   - Once the turkey is cooked, remove it from the pan and set it aside to rest. Pour the drippings from the roasting pan into a saucepan, straining out any solids.
   - Add the butter to the pan and melt it over medium heat. Whisk in the flour and cook for 2-3 minutes to form a roux. Gradually add the turkey stock and apple cider, whisking constantly until the gravy thickens. Season with salt and pepper to taste.

4. **Serve:**
   - Carve the turkey and serve with the cider gravy on the side.

Tips & Tricks:

- **Basting:** Basting the turkey with apple cider helps to keep it moist and adds a subtle sweetness to the skin.

- **Gravy Secrets:** Use a combination of turkey stock and drippings for the gravy to maximize flavor. Make sure to strain the drippings to remove any impurities before making the gravy.

- **Resting the Turkey:** Allow the turkey to rest for at least 20 minutes before carving. This ensures the juices redistribute and the meat remains tender and moist.

Roasted Rack of Lamb with Herb Crust for Special Occasions

Rack of lamb is a dish synonymous with special occasions, and Bobby Flay's herb-crusted version is perfect for impressing your guests during a holiday feast. The lamb is roasted to perfection and coated with a mixture of fresh herbs, garlic, and mustard for a flavor-packed crust that pairs beautifully with the tender, flavorful meat.

Ingredients:

- **For the Lamb:**
    - 2 racks of lamb (8 ribs each), trimmed
    - 1 tablespoon olive oil
    - 2 tablespoons Dijon mustard
    - 3 tablespoons fresh rosemary, chopped
    - 2 tablespoons fresh thyme, chopped
    - 3 cloves garlic, minced
    - Salt and freshly ground black pepper

- **For Serving:**
  - Fresh mint leaves, chopped (optional)
  - Roasted potatoes or couscous, for serving

Preparation:

1. **Prepare the Lamb:**
   - Preheat the oven to 400°F (200°C). Rub the lamb racks with olive oil, then season with salt and pepper. Brush the Dijon mustard generously over the meat.
   - Combine the rosemary, thyme, and garlic in a small bowl, then press this herb mixture onto the mustard-coated lamb racks.

2. **Roast the Lamb:**
   - Place the lamb racks bone-side down on a roasting pan. Roast for 20-25 minutes for medium-rare, or longer for your desired doneness.
   - Rest the lamb for 10 minutes before slicing between the ribs to serve.

3. **Serve:**
   - Serve the lamb with a sprinkle of fresh mint and alongside roasted potatoes or couscous for a complete meal.

Tips & Tricks:

- **Crust Variation:** You can use a variety of herbs depending on your preference, such as tarragon, oregano, or parsley.
- **Perfect Roast Time:** Use a meat thermometer to monitor the lamb's internal temperature. For medium-rare, aim for 130°F (54°C) before resting.

- **Mint Garnish:** Fresh mint enhances the lamb's flavor, but you can also serve it with a mint yogurt sauce for extra richness.

With these dishes, Bobby Flay offers an array of bold and creative recipes that elevate any gathering. Whether it's a roasted beef tenderloin, a stunning rack of lamb, or a show-stopping crab cake, these recipes provide the perfect balance of flavors to help you create unforgettable holiday feasts and celebrations. The tips and tricks throughout this chapter will ensure your success in recreating these meals, and Flay's personal anecdotes remind us all that cooking is about sharing the joy of great food with those we love.

Chapter 11: A Taste of Bobby Flay's Restaurants

Introduction: Bringing the Restaurant Experience Home

For Bobby Flay, his restaurants represent a collection of diverse culinary styles, each showcasing his innovative approach to food. From the bold Southwestern flavors of Mesa Grill to the refined dishes at Bar Americain, Flay's restaurants embody his philosophy of mixing the finest ingredients with creative techniques to deliver unforgettable dining experiences. His goal has always been to make the world of fine dining accessible to everyone, creating dishes that are both approachable and exciting.

In this chapter, we'll explore some of the standout recipes from Bobby Flay's restaurants, offering you a taste of what makes his establishments so special. Whether you're recreating the vibrant flavors of Mesa Grill's Grilled Corn Salad, savoring the richness of Duck Confit from Bar Americain, or indulging in the comfort of Gato's Ricotta Gnudi, these recipes bring the restaurant experience straight to your kitchen. Each dish has been carefully crafted to offer a perfect balance of flavors, textures, and presentation—just like the dishes served at Bobby Flay's restaurants.

These recipes are designed not just to impress but also to teach you the techniques behind the food that Flay's restaurants are known for. We'll dive into the inspiration behind each dish, explore the key ingredients, and provide tips and tricks to help you perfect them in your own kitchen.

Mesa Grill's Signature Grilled Corn Salad

Grilled Corn Salad is one of the most iconic dishes at Mesa Grill, embodying Bobby Flay's love for Southwestern flavors. The smokiness of the grilled corn, combined with a tangy dressing and fresh vegetables, creates a dish that's as vibrant as it is flavorful. This salad is perfect as a side dish for any meal but also makes a great main course when paired with a protein like grilled chicken or steak.

Ingredients:

- 4 ears of corn, husked and grilled
- 1/2 cup red bell pepper, diced
- 1/2 cup red onion, finely chopped
- 1/4 cup cilantro, chopped
- 1/4 cup cotija cheese, crumbled (or feta cheese as a substitute)
- 1/4 cup extra virgin olive oil
- 2 tablespoons fresh lime juice
- 1 tablespoon red vinegar vinegar
- 1 teaspoon ground cumin
- Salt and freshly ground black pepper to taste
- 1 small jalapeño, seeds removed, finely chopped (optional for heat)

Preparation:

1. **Grill the Corn:**

   o Preheat the grill to medium-high heat. Place the corn directly on the grill and cook for about 10 minutes, turning occasionally, until the kernels are slightly charred and tender.

   o Remove the corn from the grill and allow it to cool for a few minutes before cutting the kernels off the cob using a sharp knife.

2. **Prepare the Salad:**

   o In a large mixing bowl, combine the grilled corn, red bell pepper, red onion, cilantro, and cotija cheese. If you like a little heat, add the chopped jalapeño.

3. **Make the Dressing:**

   o In a small bowl, whisk together the olive oil, lime juice, red vinegar vinegar, cumin, salt, and pepper.

4. **Assemble the Salad:**

   o Pour the dressing over the salad and toss everything together gently. Taste and adjust seasoning as needed, adding more salt, lime juice, or vinegar if desired.

5. **Serve:**

   o Serve the salad at room temperature or chilled. It pairs wonderfully with grilled meats or can be enjoyed on its own for a refreshing, satisfying dish.

Tips & Tricks:

- **Grilling Corn:** Make sure to grill the corn until you see a bit of charring. This gives the salad a smoky flavor that's essential to the dish.

- **Cheese Alternatives:** If you can't find cotija cheese, feta works as a good substitute, providing a similar salty, crumbly texture.

- **Add More Veggies:** Feel free to add more veggies such as diced tomatoes, zucchini, or avocado for added freshness and texture.

Bar Americain's Duck Confit with Apricot Glaze

Duck confit is one of the most luxurious and flavorful dishes you can serve, and Bobby Flay's rendition at Bar Americain is no exception. Slow-cooked to perfection, the duck is incredibly tender, and the apricot glaze adds a perfect balance of sweetness and acidity. This dish is an excellent choice for special occasions, and it's a perfect way to impress your guests with your cooking skills.

Ingredients:

- **For the Duck Confit:**

  o 4 duck legs (with thighs)

  o 4 cups duck fat (enough to submerge the duck legs)

- o 4 garlic cloves, smashed
- o 2 sprigs fresh thyme
- o 1 tablespoon black peppercorns
- o 1 teaspoon salt

- **For the Apricot Glaze:**
  - o 1/2 cup apricot preserves
  - o 1/4 cup apple cider vinegar
  - o 1 tablespoon Dijon mustard
  - o 1/2 teaspoon ground ginger
  - o Salt and pepper to taste

Preparation:

1. **Prepare the Duck:**
   - o Preheat your oven to 275°F (135°C). Season the duck legs with salt and pepper. In a large Dutch oven, melt the duck fat over low heat until it's fully liquefied. Add the garlic, thyme, and peppercorns to the fat.
   - o Submerge the duck legs in the duck fat, cover the Dutch oven, and place it in the oven. Let the duck cook slowly for 2 to 3 hours until the meat is tender and can easily be pulled from the bone.

2. **Make the Apricot Glaze:**
   - o While the duck is cooking, prepare the glaze by combining the apricot preserves, apple cider vinegar, Dijon mustard, ginger, salt, and pepper in a small saucepan. Bring to a simmer over medium heat, stirring occasionally. Let the glaze reduce for about 10 minutes, until it thickens slightly.

3. **Crisp the Duck:**

- Once the duck is fully cooked, remove it from the fat and pat the legs dry with paper towels. Heat a large skillet over medium-high heat and add a little oil. When the pan is hot, sear the duck legs skin-side down for 4-5 minutes until the skin is crispy and golden brown.

4. **Glaze the Duck:**

   - Brush the apricot glaze over the duck legs, making sure to coat them evenly. Let the glaze caramelize in the pan for another 2-3 minutes.

5. **Serve:**

   - Serve the duck confit hot, drizzling with extra apricot glaze if desired. This dish pairs beautifully with mashed potatoes or a simple green vegetable like sautéed spinach.

Tips & Tricks:

- **Duck Fat:** Duck fat is key to achieving tender, flavorful duck confit. If you can't find it, you can use a mix of olive oil and vegetable oil, but duck fat is ideal.

- **Crisping the Skin:** Make sure the duck skin is dry before you sear it to get the crispiest, most delicious result.

- **Glaze Adjustments:** If you prefer a less sweet glaze, you can reduce the amount of apricot preserves or add a little more vinegar to balance out the flavors.

Gato's Ricotta Gnudi with Sage Brown Butter

Ricotta gnudi is a delicious and delicate dish that's a perfect representation of Bobby Flay's more refined approach to Italian cooking. At Gato, the gnudi are served with a rich and nutty sage brown butter, creating a dish that's comforting yet elegant. This recipe is a beautiful balance of textures—the lightness of the ricotta gnudi paired with the richness of the butter sauce.

Ingredients:

- **For the Gnudi:**
    - 1 1/2 cups fresh ricotta cheese
    - 1/2 cup all-purpose flour
    - 1/4 cup grated Parmesan cheese
    - 1 large egg
    - 1/4 teaspoon nutmeg
    - Salt and pepper to taste
- **For the Sage Brown Butter:**
    - 1/2 cup unsalted butter
    - 12 fresh sage leaves
    - Salt to taste

Preparation:

1. **Make the Gnudi:**
    - In a mixing bowl, combine the ricotta, flour, Parmesan, egg, nutmeg, salt, and pepper. Mix until the dough comes together. If it's too wet, add a little more flour until it's workable.
    - Roll the dough into small balls, about 1 inch in diameter. Lightly dust them with flour and set them aside on a tray.
2. **Cook the Gnudi:**
    - Bring a large pot of salted water to a boil. Gently drop the gnudi into the water, cooking in batches. Once the gnudi float to the surface (about 2-3 minutes), remove them with a slotted spoon and set aside.

3. **Make the Sage Brown Butter:**

   ○ In a large skillet, melt the butter over medium heat. Add the sage leaves and cook for 2-3 minutes until the butter begins to brown and the sage crisps up. Be careful not to burn the butter.

4. **Combine and Serve:**

   ○ Add the cooked gnudi to the skillet with the sage brown butter and toss gently to coat. Season with salt to taste and serve hot.

Tips & Tricks:

- **Texture of the Gnudi:** The key to light, fluffy gnudi is to use fresh ricotta and not overwork the dough. If the mixture feels too sticky, add a little more flour.

- **Brown Butter:** Watch the butter closely as it browns; you want it to develop a nutty flavor, but you don't want it to burn. The sage leaves add a wonderful earthy flavor, so make sure they crisp up.

- **Gnudi Variations:** You can experiment with different herbs or cheeses in the gnudi mixture. Try adding some fresh basil or swapping Parmesan for Pecorino for a sharper flavor.

This chapter captures the essence of Bobby Flay's restaurants, bringing some of his signature dishes into your home. Whether it's the smoky, refreshing Mesa Grill Grilled Corn Salad or the rich, decadent Duck Confit from Bar Americain, each recipe is a journey through Flay's innovative culinary mind. With a little guidance and some practice, you'll be able to recreate these restaurant-quality dishes in your own kitchen and impress your guests with flavors from Bobby Flay's restaurants.

Chapter 12: Flay's Culinary Philosophy

Introduction: Bobby Flay's Approach to Cooking

Bobby Flay's approach to cooking is rooted in a deep passion for flavors, techniques, and, most importantly, the joy of creating food that brings people together. His philosophy is all about balancing bold flavors, embracing fresh ingredients, and presenting food in a way that not only pleases the taste buds but also delights the eyes. Over the course of his illustrious career, Flay has transformed the way we think about American cuisine, introducing bold, layered flavors from around the world into the fabric of modern cooking. But at the heart of it all is his commitment to simplicity, authenticity, and respect for the ingredients he works with.

For Bobby Flay, cooking isn't just about preparing food; it's about creating an experience that transcends the plate. He believes that cooking should be about connecting with others, telling stories through food, and expressing one's unique voice in the kitchen. This chapter delves into Bobby Flay's culinary philosophy, examining the principles that guide his cooking style and offering insight into how home cooks can incorporate these ideas into their own kitchens. With personal anecdotes and insights, we will explore the foundational elements of his approach, from building flavors to the role of confidence in the kitchen. Each section will provide practical tips, tricks, and techniques that can elevate your cooking and deepen your appreciation for the art of making great food.

The Power of Bold, Layered Flavors

One of the hallmarks of Bobby Flay's cooking is his ability to create dishes with bold, layered flavors that resonate with complexity. Flay believes that food should never be one-dimensional. Instead, it should be an orchestra of tastes, textures, and aromas that harmonize on the palate, creating a memorable dining experience. For Flay, achieving bold flavors is not about relying on heavy-handed seasoning or overwhelming the dish with spice;

rather, it's about building flavor from the ground up—starting with quality ingredients and using techniques that enhance their natural qualities.

Flay often draws inspiration from his travels and his love of global cuisines. He's particularly influenced by the vibrant, bold flavors of Southwestern, Mediterranean, and Latin American cuisines, where the use of fresh herbs, citrus, chiles, and spices creates a depth of flavor that's both layered and intricate. However, he adapts these influences to fit within his unique culinary voice, taking inspiration from tradition but never shying away from innovation.

Creating Layers of Flavor

To create bold, layered flavors, Flay recommends focusing on the following techniques:

1. **Building Depth with Base Ingredients:**
   - Start with a strong base. Whether you're making a sauce, a marinade, or a soup, the foundation is crucial. Roasting vegetables, sautéing aromatics like onions, garlic, and ginger, or browning meats creates a depth of flavor that will carry throughout the dish.
   - Flay emphasizes the importance of developing flavors through technique. For example, when preparing a sauce, he suggests letting it simmer to develop complexity. Don't rush the process—flavors often need time to fully come together.

2. **Layering Flavors with Fresh Ingredients:**
   - Fresh ingredients play a significant role in achieving depth in a dish. Flay is known for using vibrant herbs, citrus zest, and fresh produce to bring brightness and complexity to his recipes. He believes that fresh ingredients should be treated with respect, allowing them to shine rather than overpowering them with heavy seasoning.
   - A perfect example of layering fresh ingredients can be found in Flay's *Shrimp and Avocado Salad*, where the sweetness of the shrimp is balanced with the creaminess of the avocado, the acidity

of the lime, and the heat from jalapeños, all of which come together to create a balanced, yet bold flavor profile.

3. **Balancing Acidity and Heat:**

   o Acidity and heat are two powerful tools in Flay's flavor arsenal. A squeeze of fresh lime or a splash of vinegar can brighten and elevate a dish, while the right amount of heat from chiles or spices adds intensity and complexity.

   o For example, in his *Grilled Tuna with Soy-Ginger Marinade*, Flay combines the umami-rich flavors of soy sauce with the heat of ginger and the sharpness of lime to create a marinade that brings the fish to life.

Practical Tips for Achieving Bold Flavors:

- **Layering Spices:** Start with a base spice (like cumin or paprika), then add heat (like chili powder or cayenne) and finish with fresh herbs or citrus for balance.

- **Don't Fear Salt:** Salt is a key player in balancing and bringing out the flavors in a dish. Taste as you go and adjust seasoning at every stage of cooking.

- **Build Depth with Cooking Techniques:** Use techniques like roasting, searing, and braising to create flavors that develop over time. Slow cooking can be particularly effective for bringing out deep, rich flavors in meats and vegetables.

The Importance of Fresh Ingredients

At the heart of Bobby Flay's cooking is his unwavering commitment to using fresh, high-quality ingredients. Whether it's the vibrant produce from a farmer's market, freshly caught seafood, or locally sourced meats, Flay believes that fresh ingredients are the foundation of great cooking. He often says, "If you start with the best ingredients, the dish almost cooks itself."

Fresh ingredients are not only important for flavor but also for texture, color, and nutritional value. Flay is a firm believer that ingredients should be treated with respect, and that starts with sourcing them from local purveyors or growing them yourself. The fresher the ingredient, the less you need to do to it. Great ingredients can shine with minimal intervention, and it's through this approach that many of Flay's dishes come to life.

Flay's Approach to Sourcing Ingredients

- **Locally Sourced Produce:** Flay encourages home cooks to seek out locally grown, seasonal produce whenever possible. By using fruits and vegetables that are in season, you're able to enjoy them at their peak of flavor. For example, Flay's *Tomato-Cucumber Salad* makes the most of summer's bounty, with fresh tomatoes and cucumbers paired with a light vinaigrette.

- **Fresh Seafood and Meats:** Flay is known for his affinity for seafood, particularly fresh fish and shellfish. When working with seafood, he stresses the importance of freshness and sustainability. For a dish like *Lobster Tacos with Avocado and Chipotle-Lime Crema*, using fresh lobster is crucial to achieving the perfect balance of sweetness and richness in the dish.

- **Herbs and Spices:** Fresh herbs are an essential component in Flay's cooking. Whether it's basil, cilantro, mint, or thyme, fresh herbs bring brightness and complexity to dishes. He recommends using herbs at the end of the cooking process to preserve their fresh flavor.

Tips for Working with Fresh Ingredients:

- **Seasonality:** Learn what's in season in your region. Seasonal produce is typically fresher, more flavorful, and less expensive.

- **Buy in Small Batches:** If possible, buy fresh ingredients in smaller quantities so that you can use them while they're still at their peak freshness.

- **Minimize Waste:** Use every part of the ingredient. For example, you can use herb stems for stocks or garnishes, or vegetable peels for making broths.

Cooking with Confidence and Passion

For Bobby Flay, cooking is a form of self-expression, and the key to great cooking lies in confidence and passion. He believes that cooking should be a joyful experience, and it's that passion that drives him to create memorable dishes. Flay's confidence in the kitchen comes from years of experience, trial and error, and a deep understanding of flavors and techniques.

Confidence in the kitchen doesn't mean cooking without mistakes; it means trusting your instincts and being open to experimentation. Flay encourages home cooks to trust their senses—taste the food, feel the texture, and adjust as you go. Cooking is an evolving process, and it's okay to change a dish as you go along if something doesn't feel quite right.

Flay's Advice on Building Confidence:

1. **Start with Simple Dishes:**

   o If you're new to cooking, begin with simple recipes that allow you to build your skills. Flay's *Smoked Tomato and Bacon Soup* is a great beginner recipe that introduces you to flavor layering without being overwhelming.

2. **Embrace Mistakes:**

   o Flay is quick to acknowledge that even the most experienced chefs make mistakes in the kitchen. The key is to learn from them and not be afraid to try new things.

3. **Use Your Senses:**

   o Trust your senses when cooking. Taste frequently, feel the texture of meats and vegetables, and adjust seasoning along the way. Cooking is a fluid process, and it's important to stay connected to the food you're preparing.

Seasoning and Saucing: Mastering the Basics

Seasoning and saucing are two fundamental aspects of Bobby Flay's cooking that can make or break a dish. Seasoning enhances and balances the flavors, while sauces add richness and complexity. Flay believes that understanding how to properly season and sauce your dishes is key to elevating your cooking to the next level.

Flay's Tips for Seasoning:

1. **Season at Every Stage:**

   o Don't wait until the end to season your food. Season as you go—add salt and pepper at different stages of cooking to build layers of flavor. Flay suggests tasting frequently and adjusting the seasoning as you go along.

2. **Balancing Flavors:**

   o Seasoning isn't just about salt and pepper. Flay encourages using a variety of spices and seasonings to balance flavors. Sweet, sour, salty, and bitter elements all play a role in creating harmony in your dish.

Flay's Saucing Secrets:

1. **Embrace the Sauce:**

   o Bobby Flay's sauces are often the star of his dishes. Whether it's a rich, smoky barbecue sauce or a bright, citrusy vinaigrette, sauces add an essential layer of flavor. Flay's *Chipotle Mayo* or *Cilantro Pesto* are perfect examples of how a great sauce can elevate a dish.

2. **The Right Consistency:**

   o A sauce should complement the dish, not overwhelm it. Flay stresses the importance of adjusting the consistency of your sauces to suit the dish. For example, a thick sauce might work well with grilled meats, while a lighter vinaigrette might be perfect for fresh salads.

The Art of Plating and Presentation

Bobby Flay's dishes are as visually striking as they are delicious. For Flay, plating is an art form—a way to present food that's both aesthetically pleasing and functional. He believes that the way food is presented can enhance the overall dining experience, creating a sense of anticipation and excitement before the first bite.

Flay's Plating Tips:

1. **Keep It Simple:**
   - Flay's plating style is clean and elegant. He advises keeping things simple and focusing on the natural beauty of the ingredients. Use white plates to create contrast, and avoid overcrowding the dish with too many elements.

2. **Balance and Harmony:**
   - When plating, Flay focuses on creating balance and harmony between the different components of the dish. The placement of the proteins, vegetables, and sauces should feel intentional, with each element complementing the others.

3. **Use Color and Texture:**
   - Colorful vegetables, fresh herbs, and contrasting textures add vibrancy to the plate. Flay often incorporates crispy elements like fried herbs or breadcrumbs to add a playful texture that contrasts with creamy or tender components.

Conclusion: A Legacy of Flavors

Bobby Flay's culinary philosophy is a testament to his passion for food, his creativity, and his dedication to excellence. From building bold, layered flavors to cooking with confidence and presenting food in an artful way, Flay's approach is grounded in respect for ingredients and a deep understanding of what makes food truly special. By embracing his philosophy and following the tips and techniques shared throughout this chapter, you can create your own culinary masterpieces and elevate your cooking to new heights. Whether you're a beginner or an experienced cook, Flay's philosophy offers valuable lessons that will guide you every step of the way, helping you create dishes that are as delicious as they are memorable.

Chapter 13: A Future of Flavor

Introduction: What's Next for Bobby Flay

Bobby Flay is undoubtedly one of the most influential chefs in contemporary American cuisine. Over the decades, he has redefined what it means to be a celebrity chef, establishing a culinary empire that includes award-winning restaurants, television shows, cookbooks, and a legion of fans who admire not only his cooking but his approach to food. As Bobby Flay looks to the future, he continues to evolve, embracing new flavors, ingredients, and techniques that keep his cooking fresh and exciting.

In this chapter, we will explore what lies ahead for Bobby Flay, diving into his thoughts on the future of food, his plans for upcoming culinary ventures, and the evolution of his signature cooking style. We will also take a look at some of the ideas that have influenced his success over the years, including his passion for bold, layered flavors, his adaptability in a changing culinary landscape, and his ability to connect with a broader audience.

In addition to looking at the future, this chapter will reflect on some of Flay's personal experiences and philosophies, offering insight into what has driven his success and what continues to inspire him as he pushes forward into the next chapter of his career.

Flay's Secret Ingredient: The Spice of Life

If there's one thing Bobby Flay is known for, it's his ability to transform dishes with the addition of bold spices. His cooking is often defined by a keen understanding of how to use spices—not just for heat, but for the depth, complexity, and vibrancy they bring to the dish. For Flay, spices are a way to awaken the senses and elevate even the simplest ingredients into something extraordinary.

Flay's love affair with spices is not just about heat—although he certainly enjoys the kick of a good chili pepper—but about balance, harmony, and the careful layering of flavors. He often speaks of his first exposure to the bold flavors of Southwestern cuisine as a transformative experience, one that shaped his approach to cooking and inspired him to experiment with flavors in ways that were unconventional at the time.

His secret ingredient, however, is not just one spice—it's a collection of spices, herbs, and seasonings that come together to form a vibrant palate of flavors. Flay's style is about the interplay between ingredients, using spices to enhance the natural qualities of the dish. From smoky chipotles to fragrant cumin and zesty lime, the ability to blend spices to create a harmonious, well-rounded flavor profile is central to Bobby Flay's culinary genius.

Flay's Spice Staples:

- **Chipotle:** Flay's go-to for smoky, earthy heat. Whether in a salsa, a marinade, or a dry rub, chipotle is a signature ingredient that gives many of Flay's dishes their trademark warmth and smokiness.

- **Cumin:** Known for its nutty, warm flavor, cumin is often used in Flay's Southwestern and Mediterranean dishes. It pairs well with beans, meats, and vegetables, and is a perfect complement to dishes that require depth and earthiness.

- **Smoked Paprika:** A favorite of Flay's, smoked paprika brings a sweet, smoky flavor to a variety of dishes. It's used in everything from his signature grilled vegetables to rubs for meats and seafood.

- **Lime:** While not technically a spice, lime is an essential part of Flay's cooking philosophy. Its sharp acidity brightens up dishes and balances the richness of meats, seafood, and creamy ingredients. It's frequently used in his marinades and dressings.

How to Use Spices like Bobby Flay:

1. **Layering Flavors:** Start with spices that form a base, such as cumin or smoked paprika, and build layers with more aromatic spices like coriander or cinnamon. Add fresh ingredients like citrus or herbs for balance and brightness.

2. **Toasting Spices:** Flay often recommends toasting spices in a dry pan to bring out their essential oils and intensify their flavor. This step is particularly effective with cumin, coriander, and mustard seeds.

3. **Heat Management:** When working with hot spices, it's important to manage the heat. Flay suggests using milder peppers, like Anaheim or poblano, for a more subtle heat, while jalapeños or chipotles can add a more pronounced punch.

Cooking in the Digital Age: TV, Books, and Beyond

Bobby Flay has been at the forefront of culinary television for decades. His shows, from *Grill It! with Bobby Flay* to *Iron Chef America* and *Throwdown with Bobby Flay*, have not only showcased his cooking skills but also made him a household name. His ability to connect with viewers and teach them about food in an approachable way has been a key factor in his success in the digital age.

As food media has evolved, so too has Flay's role in the culinary world. In an age where digital platforms have become essential for chefs to connect with their audience, Flay has adapted seamlessly, expanding his brand beyond television to include social media, YouTube, and a successful online business. He has been able to use digital platforms to showcase his cooking philosophy, share new recipes, and connect with his growing fanbase.

Flay's Television Legacy:

- **Iron Chef America:** One of Flay's most notable roles was as a competitor and later, a host, on *Iron Chef America*. His time on the show helped to elevate his profile as a culinary expert and established him as one of the top chefs in the country.

- **Throwdown with Bobby Flay:** This show exemplified Flay's competitive spirit and allowed him to interact with home cooks and fellow chefs, showcasing his culinary creativity and adaptability.

- **Digital Platforms:** Flay has embraced platforms like Instagram, YouTube, and his own website to share his culinary knowledge. His online presence allows fans and aspiring chefs to learn from him directly, whether through recipe videos, behind-the-scenes glimpses, or cooking tips.

Flay's Evolving Role in Food Media:

Flay's involvement in food media has also expanded to include cookbooks, with each one providing a deeper insight into his cooking philosophy. His books serve as a valuable resource for aspiring chefs, home cooks, and fans alike, offering step-by-step guides, tips, and personal anecdotes.

Flay has also become a prominent voice in the food world beyond cooking. He is an advocate for sustainable practices, using his platform to promote responsible sourcing, reducing food waste, and supporting local food systems. As the culinary world becomes more connected through digital media, Flay's role as both an educator and advocate will continue to evolve.

The Evolution of Flay's Signature Style

Bobby Flay's signature cooking style has evolved considerably over the years. Initially known for his bold Southwestern flavors, he expanded his repertoire to include Mediterranean influences, Asian flavors, and more modern American dishes. Through this evolution, Flay has maintained his commitment to fresh ingredients, bold spices, and dishes that emphasize flavor and creativity.

While his early dishes were heavily influenced by the bold flavors of the Southwest, Flay's culinary style has grown to include a variety of global influences, from Latin American and Mediterranean to Asian and beyond. His ability to blend these diverse flavors while maintaining a sense of balance and freshness has become one of his defining characteristics.

Flay's Evolving Flavor Palette:

- **Southwestern Roots:** Flay's early career was defined by his love for Southwestern flavors, particularly those of Mexican and Tex-Mex cuisine. Over time, he expanded his focus to incorporate a broader range of flavors, but the bold, smoky, and spicy elements from this region remain a cornerstone of his cooking.

- **Mediterranean and Asian Influences:** As Flay traveled more and explored different cuisines, he began incorporating Mediterranean and Asian flavors into his cooking. His *Grilled Mediterranean Octopus with Olive Tapenade* and *Thai Beef Salad with Lime and Thai Basil* are perfect examples of this fusion of influences, blending the flavors of the Mediterranean and Asia in innovative ways.

- **Modern American Twist:** Today, Flay's dishes are a reflection of the diversity of American cuisine. He embraces ingredients and techniques from around the world but always with a distinctly American perspective. His *BBQ Short Ribs with Roasted Garlic Mashed Potatoes* and *Grilled Herb-Crusted Rack of Lamb* are great examples of how Flay puts his own spin on American classics.

Bobby Flay's Dream Dish

Throughout his career, Bobby Flay has created countless dishes that have become iconic in the culinary world. But what is his ultimate dream dish? According to Flay, it's not necessarily about creating something entirely new, but about creating a dish that captures the essence of who he is as a chef.

Flay has expressed a love for simple, rustic dishes that highlight the flavors of fresh, high-quality ingredients. His dream dish, then, would likely be something that celebrates his roots in Southwestern cuisine while incorporating some of the bold, global flavors he's embraced over the years. Whether it's a perfectly grilled steak, a seafood dish featuring fresh lobster, or a vibrant vegetable salad with layers of spice and acidity, his dream dish would bring together everything he's learned and loved about food.

What's On the Horizon: Looking to the Next Chapter

As Bobby Flay continues to evolve, his culinary journey is far from over. He has several exciting ventures on the horizon, both in the restaurant world and in food media. With new restaurant concepts, potential television projects, and a growing presence in the digital space, the future looks incredibly bright for Flay.

One of the things Flay is most excited about is the continued evolution of his restaurant concepts. As the food world continues to shift, Flay is excited to explore new ways of connecting with diners, offering fresh experiences, and continuing to innovate in the kitchen.

Conclusion

Bobby Flay's culinary journey has been defined by his passion for bold flavors, his ability to adapt to new trends, and his commitment to elevating American cuisine. As he looks to the future, Flay's influence in the culinary world is only set to grow. With his focus on fresh ingredients, creative flavor combinations, and a deep understanding of what makes food truly great, Bobby Flay's legacy will continue to inspire chefs and food lovers for generations to come.

As you embark on your own culinary journey, remember that it's not just about the recipes—it's about the passion, the creativity, and the love for food that drives every dish. With Bobby Flay's philosophy as a guide, the future of cooking is bright, flavorful, and full of endless possibilities.

Made in the USA
Las Vegas, NV
27 December 2024

15418693R00074